South
Toward Home

South Toward Home

Travels in Southern Literature

MARGARET EBY

W. W. Norton & Company

Independent Publishers Since 1923

New York • London

For information about permission to reproduce selections from
this book, write to Permissions, W. W. Norton & Company, Inc.,
500 Fifth Avenue, New York, NY 10110

For information about special discounts for bulk purchases, please
contact W. W. Norton Special Sales at specialsales@wwnorton.com
or 800-233-4830

Manufacturing by Quad Graphics Fairfield
Book design by Mary Austin Speaker
Production manager: Julia Druskin

Library of Congress Cataloging-in-Publication Data

Eby, Margaret.
South toward home : travels in Southern literature / Margaret
Eby.—1st ed.
    pages cm
Includes bibliographical references.
ISBN 978-0-393-24111-2 (hardcover)
1. American literature—Southern States—History and criticism.
2. Authors, American—Homes and haunts—Southern States.
3. Southern States—In literature. 4. Southern States—Social life
and customs. 5. Southern States—Intellectual life. I. Title.
PS261.E39 2015
810.9'975—dc23

                            2015013986

W. W. Norton & Company, Inc.
500 Fifth Avenue, New York, N.Y. 10110
www.wwnorton.com

W. W. Norton & Company Ltd.
Castle House, 75/76 Wells Street, London W1T 3QT

1 2 3 4 5 6 7 8 9 0

For Tom, Mary, Brendan, and Conor,
my first and best traveling companions

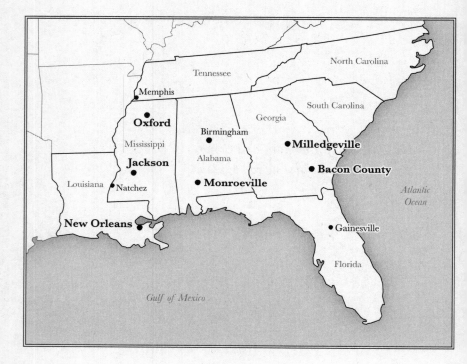

Tennessee

North Carolina

Memphis

South Carolina

Oxford

Mississippi

Birmingham

Georgia

Milledgeville

Alabama

Jackson

Bacon County

Louisiana

Natchez

Monroeville

Atlantic Ocean

New Orleans

Gainesville

Florida

Gulf of Mexico

Contents

Introduction

The South is vast. Depending on how you draw the boundaries, it can stretch clear up from Florida to Maryland, and all the way over to Texas, and can include everything from the Appalachians to the Pineywoods. No wonder that the literary output of the place contains multitudes.

And yet there is *something* about writers from the South. There is a certain flavor to Southern literature that distinguishes it from other regional writing, a ferocity about it, which is why William Faulkner and Flannery O'Connor and Richard Wright and Harper Lee and so many others are not known just as American writers, but Southern writers. There is no popular category known as Northern literature. And thus the perennial interview question for fiction writers who grapple with characters below the Mason-Dixon: What is it about the place that inspires so many? What makes the South different?

There are stock answers, ones about storytelling traditions and the defeat and alienation of the Civil War and small-town customs, yarns about grits and ghosts.

They all brush the truth, but never quite grasp it. There's a line in *Absalom, Absalom!* that acts partially as Faulkner's reply to that question. Mississippian Quentin Compson finds himself unable to answer his Harvard roommate Shreve when pestered to talk about his home. "What is it?" Shreve asks. "Something you live and breathe in like air? a kind of vacuum filled with wraithlike and indomitable anger and pride and glory at and in happenings that occurred and ceased fifty years ago?" Quentin, exasperated, eventually replies: "You can't understand it. You would have to be born there."

It's a good line, but it's not true. The best writers of Southern fiction prove that, by conveying exactly what the place is like to the people who aren't born there. Southern writing at its loftiest is a literature of opposition. It is a rebuff, in equal measure, to those who imagine the region as a place full of shoeless yokels, and those who mythologize it as one where sweet-faced, big-haired debutantes in hoop skirts dole out petits fours, mind their manners, and maintain deep roots to their family elders. The popular image of the South is of a monolithic, defeated country, some melee of swamps, magnolia trees, and antebellum houses populated by rifle-toting, camouflage-wearing fundamentalists and sneering good ole boys scored to menacing banjo music, something like H. L. Mencken's 1917 essay "The Sahara of the Bozart," in which he declared the South to be "almost as sterile, artistically, intellectually, culturally" as the famous desert ("Bozart" was a play on the

Southern pronunciation of "beaux arts"). Often these clichés, what Barry Hannah described as the "canned dream of the South," are blamed on Northerners with a faint idea of the South. (As Flannery O'Connor complained, "I have found that anything that comes out of the South is going to be called grotesque by the Northern reader, unless it is grotesque, in which case it's going to be called realistic.") But really, these clichés are manufactured and perpetuated by Southerners and Northerners alike. That's why boutiques in Mississippi, Alabama, Georgia, and South Carolina all carry signs with some variation on the saying "In the South we don't hide crazy: We sit it on the porch and bring it sweet tea!" The aim of these writers' work is to dismantle the stereotypes of what it means to be from Alabama or Mississippi or Louisiana, what it's like to live there at a certain time, in certain social circumstances.

Books like Richard Wright's *Black Boy* or Harry Crews's *A Childhood* counter the sweeping generalizations about the South by being unrelentingly specific about one place. Faulkner did not write about the South generally; he wrote about Oxford, Mississippi, particularly. Ditto Eudora Welty and Jackson, John Kennedy Toole and New Orleans, and so on. Their writing is also an act of preservation, to document what it is, exactly, that distinguishes the two-gas-station hamlets in Alabama from the rest of America. What makes a Southern writer a Southern writer is not just the circumstances of his or her birth but a fierce attachment to a particular place, and a commitment to exploring its limits in his or her work. These explorations are not universally flattering; in fact, they are mostly ambivalent. Sometimes, despite these unflattering portraits, the residents of these places came to be equally as devoted to the writers as the writers were to the place. By focusing on the minutiae of a town, the writer's work becomes a part of the well of local lore they draw from.

It's this smattering of towns across the Deep South that inspired this book, a pilgrimage to the places that a group of Southern writers described in their fiction. I was not born in the South, but I grew up there, and came to understand my identity as an Alabamian from people like O'Connor, Faulkner, and Welty. I wanted to see the places they had lived in and written about, to breathe the same air, to hear the same accents and meet the same people. I wanted to see if there were physical traces of the locations that these writers drew from, and how much they had changed, how much the actual place matched the idea I had from their fiction. Plenty of these writers cite preservation as one of the motives for keeping their fiction contained locally, an urge to document the unique proclivities of a place as it was before the forces of global capitalism take over, replacing the mom-and-pop stores with big-box chains. But every American city is subject to those same forces, and it isn't as if the South was some Eden recently ruined by McDonald's and Denny's. Part of this journey was to see what was missing, to have some sense of what parts of the South as described were worth keeping and what better to let go.

My selection of writers to cover is a personal one. There are, of course, many other excellent and worthy scribes who populate the South, and still more who had to relocate in order to further or even start their careers. There is Yazoo City, Mississippi, denizen Willie Morris, whose warm, evocative memoir about his childhood and eventual move to New York City, *North Toward Home*, served as inspiration for this book's title. There is Carson McCullers, whose Columbus, Georgia, childhood home now annually houses writers in residence. There is Zora Neale Hurston, Katherine Anne Porter, Tennessee Williams, Walker Percy, Ellen Douglas, Shelby Foote, Margaret Walker Alexander, and James Agee, to name a few from a long list. And those are just the dead ones.

But this book is not meant to be an encyclopedia of Southern literature, nor is it a travel guide. It is an odyssey of sorts through a pocket of the South that I grew up in and learned to understand through reading. Other writers would have drawn a different map, taken different pit stops, sought out different roadside shrines. The ten writers on this journey are an idiosyncratic group, but they are the ones who spoke to me most insistently as I tried to figure out what it meant to be from the South, to answer that echoing question, *What is it about this place, exactly?* They each appealed to me because of their relationship to their homes, the truth of a place that is sometimes only available through fiction. All rejected the visions of the South presented to them, the costume shop version of Southern-ness that didn't jibe with their understanding of their surroundings. I decided to borrow the same liberty. These writers, from Welty to Hannah, are all telling about their own corner of the South, and I set off to listen.

South
Toward Home

1.   Eudora Welty's Garden
JACKSON, MS

My first stop is in Jackson, Mississippi, the hometown of the masterful short-fiction writer Eudora Welty, where she was, as she put it, "locally underfoot" for most of her life. "It's where I live and look around me—it's my piece of the world—it teaches me," Welty told Alice Walker. "It's just a piece of everything that happens to be my sample."

EUDORA WELTY, or "Miss Eudora" as native Jacksonites affectionately call their literary patron saint, was a fixture in the capital city of Mississippi from her 1910s childhood until her death in 2001. Her presence is still inescapable. Visit the Mayflower Cafe, off Capitol Street, and you'll hear about Miss Eudora's fondness for plate lunches of fried catfish and butter beans. Visit Bill's Greek Tavern and you can trace more of Welty's culinary indulgences, and Bill Matheos himself will tell you about Welty attending his daughter's wedding as a guest of honor. If you were to dig through the waist-high stacks of material at the now-defunct Choctaw Books, with luck, you might come across a volume signed in Welty's bunched and looping hand. Welty used to stop into Choctaw on occasion to collect another stack of murder mysteries, a genre she particularly adored. Her neighbors will recall the informal system fans had for obtaining signed books: leave them on Welty's stoop and collect them, inscribed with a note from Miss Eudora, the next day.

The main branch of the Jackson Public Library, named in Welty's honor, has a banner with a portrait of her gentle, toothily smiling face hanging above the entrance. If you catch them in an off moment, the librarians will tell you about how Welty, as a nine-year-old girl frothed with petticoats, used to roller-skate into the former location of the branch to scoop up her allotted two books a day, how the strict librarian Miss Annie Parker could not keep enough novels in stock to satisfy Welty's literary appetite. Neighbors will smile and recount the $25 prize that Welty won in a jingle-writing contest, in which the sponsor, Mackie Pine Oil Specialty Co., sent a letter encouraging the twelve-year-old Welty to "improve in poetry to such an extent as to win fame."

Ask an alumnus of Belhaven University about Welty, and they'll tell you how, in her later years, Welty used to keep the window of her bedroom open to listen to people in the music department practice, her head just visible in the top-floor window as she sat at her typewriter. Welty's routine trips to the hairdresser down the street, and the grocery store—Jitney Jungle number 14, the etched-out sign just visible now behind the glossy neon of the local chain that bought it—became the stuff of general knowledge in the community, as well as the seeds of her fiction. Welty's story "Petrified Man" borrowed the rhythms of the gossip she heard at the salon, where she would go to get her short, curly hair fixed every week. (Her hairdresser, Miss Fanny, kept a scrapbook of Welty's hairstyles. She recently turned one hundred years old.) Welty captured the local culture around her as with a butterfly net, preserving the specimens of doddering Southern ladies and mischievous children.

Authors' homes on public display tend to have a stuffy quality, all velvet ropes and beds with hospital corners. The assiduousness of the preservation drains the life from them, makes them seem impossibly antique. But Welty's house, a Tudor-style revival tucked into a thicket of pines, is almost unbearably welcoming. "A place that ever was lived in is like a fire that never goes out," Welty wrote in "Some Notes on River Country," and you can see the spark flickering in her living room. Visiting feels like an intrusion on her privacy. The rooms are littered with paintings and clever bric-a-brac—a gaudy bust of Shakespeare on the mantel, a gold heart-shaped box inscribed with "The Ponder Heart" on a living-room table. Her many accolades—the Pulitzer Prize for *The Optimist's Daughter*, the Presidential Medal of Freedom, the National Book Award for *The Collected Works of Eudora Welty*—are sequestered in a small museum adjacent rather than hung on the walls or placed on the mantel, since Welty herself had kept them in a cardboard box tucked in the upstairs closet. Books cram into shelves in almost every room and teeter in piles on most surfaces: dictionaries, collections of Greek myths, novels by Wodehouse, Thurber, O'Connor, and Pritchett. The stone path leading to Welty's front door has one crooked stone, which she always described as looking like a false tooth.

The lived-in feeling is the result of the generosity of Welty's nieces, Mary Alice White and Elizabeth Thompson, who donated all but a few sentimental treasures back to the state when Welty died. Mary Alice, the former director of the house, who shares Welty's distinctively sloping jaw and quick wit, still occasionally leads tours of her aunt's home, reminiscing about Thanksgivings and Christmases spent in the spacious dining room. She and her sister found the house after Welty's death "slamma-jamma" with books and letters, papers pouring from the cabinets, the Kleenex scraps that Welty used as bookmarks still scattered throughout the house library. "We wanted it to still have the feeling of clutter," White told me. "We wanted it to be honest, and spontaneous." When visiting their aunt, Mary Alice and Elizabeth used to have to restack Welty's reading material just to sit down. "When I ask company to dinner I have to carry the old mail off the dining room table and hide it on my bed," Welty wrote to her friend and agent William Maxwell. "Isn't that one of the cardinal sins? Sloth I mean. I *suffer* from it."

The nieces were particularly close to their aunt, their

father having died young. Mary Alice would have Welty help with her homework, and, later, Welty taught both Mary Alice and Mary Alice's children how to drive in her Mercedes. Welty tried not to push her own work on her nieces, but Mary Alice recalled musing about a novel by Faulkner, only to have her aunt select a signed copy of the book from the wall and press it upon her. One wall of Welty's house is a floor-to-ceiling shelf that contains signed first editions from friends like Flannery O'Connor and Katherine Anne Porter, the likes of which rare-book dealers pine for. Another simply has the translations of Welty's works: *Losing Battles* in Mandarin and German, *The Optimist's Daughter* in Hebrew, French, and Italian.

Stepping into Welty's house feels less like entering another person's home than like dropping into one of her stories. Many novelists collect autobiographical details to apply to their characters, but Welty's are culled directly from her Southern surroundings. A notepad on her desk contained a list of names that she thought mellifluous enough to include, like "Miss Charlesta Culpepper (real)" and "Evergraze Hicks." Critics of Welty's writing often quibble with her penchant toward the atmospheric and the regional, concentrating on the relatively narrow scope of social life in the Deep South. (In 1943, Diana Trilling gave *Delta Wedding* a withering review in *The Nation*, describing the novel as a book in which "nothing happens," written in language that stands "on tiptoe.")

But Welty is not a regional writer—her purview is much smaller than that. Her writing is bound up in the romance of everyday objects, in the vagaries of memory and how they become tied to a place, a room, a piece of furniture, or a trinket. Welty had her own response to this claim, as she wrote in her essay "Place in Fiction":

"Regional," I think, is a careless term, as well as a condescending one, because what it does is fail to differentiate between the localized raw material of life and its outcome as art. "Regional" is an outsider's term; it has no meaning for the insider who is doing the writing, because as far as he knows he is simply writing about life.

In her house, certain objects give you literary déjà vu. There is the desk from *The Optimist's Daughter* in her bedroom, every slot filled with letters. The volumes of Dickens from *One Writer's Beginnings*, ones that Welty's mother had devoured and loved so fiercely that she threw them out the window to save them from a house fire before passing them on, are kept behind glass. A small stone carved with her parents' initials that makes an appearance in *The Optimist's Daughter* is part of the exhibit.

Welty's mother, Chestina, designed and planted the sprawling back garden when the family moved into the house in the 1920s. After Welty returned to Jackson from New York to care for her dying father, she spent most of her life weeding and watering with her mother, browsing through seed catalogues and bulb bulletins, trekking through the swamp with a bottle of snake-venom antidote at her hip to find specimens for archipelagos of flower beds and planters. With her initial earnings from the publication of her first book, Eudora screened in the side porch in order to have a shady, mosquito-sheltered place to overlook the garden. It remained until Hurricane Camille tore the screen down in 1969, leaving the brick patio shorn and bare.

When the night-blooming cereus plant ("a naked, luminous, complicated flower," Welty wrote in *The Golden Apples*) began hinting at exposing its fragile white buds each year, Welty would throw parties on her brick porch that would last from dusk until dawn in its honor. Her informal salon of friends and artists, including writers Hubert Creekmore, Frank Lyell, and Nash Burger, dubbed themselves the Night-Blooming Cereus Club. Later, the gardening team at her house was named in honor of those parties. Their shirts have the motto of Welty's club: "Don't take life too cereus. It's too mysterious."

Like her cereus parties, Welty's hostessing skills were the stuff of legend. "She was so gracious, and *funny*," Suzanne Marrs, a friend of Welty's and the author of *Eudora Welty: A Biography*, told me. "She would have the room in stitches. Just as you caught your breath, there'd be another zinger." Eudora's fast-paced joking made her a social legend, even outside her work. Her storytelling wasn't limited to the page; in fact, it seems that all the paper in the world could hardly capture the bon mots Welty threw out. If she wasn't inclined to do something, then she "would rather eat cold grits in the attic." Maker's Mark bourbon, Welty's personal favorite, flowed generously from her liquor cabinet, what she called her "entertainment center." And as ever, Welty centered the evening on a visit to the garden, tinged by moonlight or thick with the scent of the late-spring honeysuckles.

"The sight of the garden and its scent!" Welty wrote in an initial draft of *One Writer's Beginnings*. "If work hasn't proved it real, it would have been hallucination; in this sense gardening is akin to writing stories. No experience could have taught me more about grief or flowers, about achieving survival by going, young fingers in the ground, the limit of physical exhaustion." For Welty, gardening was the process that helped distill the imaginative jumble in her head into stories. It was in the garden, Welty wrote in her papers, that she first "set myself at a storyteller's remove."

Indeed, there is something botanical about Welty's work. The delicacies of her prose trick readers like Trilling into ignoring the deep roots, the hidden thorns, the sheer gumption. Her writing process was inextricable from her gardening. Both took time, patience, and nourishment. Welty and her mother spoke in the language of flowers. Weeding, Welty would remind her friends, is not an emergency. Like her method of writing—rearranging, retyping, refining—it is a slow and constant process, best approached as a habit.

Her letters to friends tracked time by what was in bloom, what plants she could see from the window of the breakfast nook. Seen through her eyes, flowers all have personalities, fashion senses, attitudes. In her correspondence, particularly to William Maxwell, it is as if Welty spun a vocabulary all her own from the horticulture. She described "oak trees in little yellow stars and epaulettes," and "buds as big as bobbins." Welty's horticultural language wasn't just complimentary. "We saw a TV performance of Judith Anderson and M. Evans in *Macbeth*," she reported to Maxwell on one occasion. "But she looked like spinach."

Camellias were Welty's particular favorite. They lined the sides of her house, pale pink or dazzling cherry red, some with names, like Berenice Boddy, that sound like small-town churchgoing folk. Welty even referred to her own moods in botanical terms, almost thinking about herself as a part of the garden. "I feel much greener," she wrote Maxwell after reading one of his stories. Like camellias, Welty suffered cold snaps and roiling humidity, both literally—"Here the thermometer jumps up & down like an ibis," she complained once—and figuratively, through the intensity of the civil rights movement and the long, painful winters of grief.

The state of the garden also tracked the ebb and flow of Welty's personal life. Welty never married, and though she had a rich social life, her main connection was with her family—her mother, Chestina, and her brothers, Edward and Walter. Welty's love life, like many of her friendships, was long-distance, conducted through absorbing, gorgeous letters. When she was in Jackson, her preoccupations were her work, a close circle of friends, and her flowers. While her mother was alive, she and Welty would tackle the garden together, gathering figs from the tree outside and coaxing new roses up from the beds. In the 1950s, as Welty's friends and family began experiencing ill health, the lavish beds were left untended. All the roses died. After her mother's death, Welty took to the garden. Nature nurtured her back to writing, comforted her in her grief.

By the 1990s, the magnificent garden had fallen into disrepair, Chestina long gone and Welty too consumed with other activities to preserve it. The once lush, multicolored sanctuary was a place of parched grass and crumbling stone benches, weeds choking whatever remained. Before Welty died in 2001, she authorized the state of Mississippi, led by preservationist and gardener Susan Haltom, to restore the garden to its former glory. The work, which Haltom documented with writer Jane Roy Brown and photographer Langdon Clay in the book *One Writer's Garden*, was painstaking. The work was simply a matter of going through seed catalogs. Many of the specimens Welty had are rare or now extinct. Haltom's goal was to approximate what the garden looked like at its peak. Her dedication to the job meant spending days in the archives, uncovering gems from Welty's house. In her study, Haltom kept a long piece of butcher paper with a map she had drawn of Welty's life: On the top, births, deaths, and love affairs. On the bottom, the writing Welty was doing, and, right up the middle, the state that the garden was in. Through the backyard, Haltom had become a cartographer of Welty's life, a biographer whose main sources were mute vines and seedpods.

Welty was an emphatically private person. She kept her struggles out of the public eye as much as possible, living a quiet life in Jackson. To her, the sum of what a reader should know was within the text. The character of Mrs. Larkin in "A Curtain of Green" is as close as she comes to self-description outside of her own essays, a mixture of Welty and Chestina, touching on her own sorrow after her father's passing, distracting herself from her grief:

> She planted every kind of flower that she could find or order from a catalogue—planted thickly and hastily, without stopping to think, without any regard for the ideas that her neighbors might elect in their club as to what constituted an appropriate vista, or an effect of restfulness, or even harmony of color.

The tiny agonies and triumphs that are the sustenance of Welty's work are all entangled in nature. But they are also, deeply and essentially, tied to the idea of home, of place. "Background matters most in how well it teaches you to look around and see clearly what's there and in how deeply it nourishes your imagination," Welty told *The Paris Review* in 1972. Jackson was the planting bed for Welty's expansive, bountiful imagination. She was a creative ambassador of her home state in a time when it was particularly difficult to defend.

Loving Jackson, and writing about it, was not an easy task in the 1950s and 1960s. As Welty wrote, various civil rights upheavals tore through the South. Fourteen-year-old Emmett Till was gruesomely killed a few hours north of where Welty would sit typing. There were the nine black students arrested in Tougaloo for reading books in a "whites only" library. The Ku Klux Klan bombed the Beth Israel synagogue, not far from Welty's house. Freedom Riders traveled on Greyhounds headed through Jackson, expecting to be met by police clubs and sneering segregationists. Except for one short story on the Medgar Evers assassination, "Where Is the Voice Coming From?," Welty rarely commented directly on these events swirling around the South. Critics disparaged her for failing to more pointedly condemn Jim Crow laws, but Welty largely ignored them. Her fiction remained untouched, though Welty did respond in her essay "Must the Novelist Crusade":

[Southern writers] do not need reminding of what our subject is. It is humankind, and we are all part of it. When we write about people, black or white, in the South or anywhere, if our stories are worth the reading, we are writing about everybody. . . . Every writer, like everybody else, thinks he's living through the crisis of the ages. To write honestly and with all our powers is the least we can do, and the most.

Welty's politics were plain: Requiring a fiction writer to respond to current events weakens their work in the long run, making it less universal. Though in smaller ways, she made her stance against segregation known, as in 1963 when she refused to speak at Millsaps, the Methodist college in Jackson, until they integrated the audience.

The only other story she wrote that explicitly addressed race, "Nicotiana," or "The Last of the Figs," Welty left unpublished. Its subject is the crotchety, bigoted Mrs. Ewing and her daughter, Sarah. The middle-aged Sarah, trapped caring for her ailing mother, eking out a living by illustrations, is an eerie reflection of Welty's own biography at the time. In "Nicotiana," there are boorish dinner party guests, troubling assessments of the "race situation," and a wayward maid with a penchant for the fruit from the fig tree outside.

Welty's preferred way of engaging with the racial injustice in her hometown was to write about every part of Mississippi, to paint a picture that included the bright spots as well as the atrocities. She extolled the beauties of

Jackson, the Delta, the swamps that she grew up in. She wrote about the lingering distrust from Reconstruction, the complicated pride that Southerners took in their Confederate heritage, the tense, quotidian interactions between races. Today, Welty scholars point to the places her fiction sprang from, speculate upon which particular neighbor was the model for which character. Mississippi was a vast reservoir of stories that Welty could draw from. As she told the interviewer from *The Paris Review*, "It's like sending a bucket down the well and it always comes up full. Wherever you go, you meet part of your story."

THE FIRST TIME I visited Eudora Welty's garden was shortly after my parents moved to Jackson, while I was in college. I had been abroad in India the whole summer as they had boxed up my childhood home in Birmingham and shipped the possessions four hours south and west into the sleepy expanse of Mississippi. When I arrived at their new house, I felt disoriented: Jackson was like Birmingham in many ways, but smudged somehow, the drawl a little deeper and the backyard clay tinged yellow instead of red. I concerned myself with rearranging familiar books on foreign shelves, taking short trips around the town to see the old Capitol Building, the fairgrounds, and the local bookstore, Lemuria, where a bust of Welty sits festooned with Mardi Gras beads.

When I got to the Welty house, one August twilight, the last tour had already gone through. I peered through the windows and looked at the brick porch, hesitating only slightly before slipping through the side trellis into the garden. The sweltering heat had died down, but the buzz of mosquitoes hung heavily in the air. I sat on a stone bench and breathed the soupy air, the humid perfume from the clumps of purple, gold, and red flowers. Something about the garden was welcoming and quiet. It made the whole of the town make a little more sense and settle in my mind.

Now I return to the garden on almost every visit. Friends come with me to stare at her trinkets; my mother accompanies me and makes sly comments on how financially difficult it is to be a full-time writer. Every tour is a little different. The docents, many of whom were Welty's neighbors and friends when she was alive, dig into their memories to tell me about her antics, how much Miss Eudora wanted her home to be an inspiration to young writers like me. I can breathe there. It feels, to me, like a place full of small and camouflaged treasures. It wasn't until later, reading through Welty's work, that I realized quite why. "One place comprehended," Welty wrote, "helps us understand all places better."

2.   Richard Wright's Schoolhouse
JACKSON, MS

The area in downtown Jackson where Richard Wright grew up isn't far from Eudora Welty's home. You can leave Welty's house on Pinehurst Street and, in less than fifteen minutes, reach the section of Jackson State University where the house Richard Wright lived with his grandparents and mother once stood. But there is no marker for Wright, no visitor center or tour guide. Wright's childhood address, 1107 John R. Lynch Street, is now part of a blank grassy lawn that rings the cheery downtown school, a historically black college where Jubilee *author Margaret Walker Alexander used to teach. Unless you knew what you were looking for, you would have no idea that one of the most influential American writers of the twentieth century had grown up there. Wright and Welty were born just a year apart, and both spent a large portion of their childhoods in Jackson. But the worlds that Welty and Wright lived in are as far apart as it is possible to be while remaining in the same town.*

THOUGH RICHARD WRIGHT grew up in Mississippi, like so many Southern black writers, he had to flee his home state in order to embark on a literary career. In his late teens, Wright started moving away from Jackson in stages, moving first to Memphis, then to Chicago and then New York and, ultimately, Paris, in order to escape the crushing racial injustice of his upbringing. By the time he was thirty-five, Wright was an international literary sensation and the first bestselling black writer in America, thanks in part to his incendiary protest novel *Native Son*, which sold at the rate of 2,000 copies a day upon publication in 1940.

But in his home state, Wright's success was not widely celebrated. Southerners met Wright's work not with ambivalence but with outright hostility. *Native Son* was banned from libraries in Birmingham, and not received much more warmly in Jackson. Where Eudora Welty was hailed as a hero, Wright was denounced as a pariah. Welty's house is a National Historic Landmark; Wright's was bulldozed. It wasn't until after Wright died that the state began to recognize his achievements and embrace him as one of their own. In 1985, fifty-eight years after the nineteen-year-old Wright left Mississippi more or less for good, the governor proclaimed a week in his honor. In 2007, the city of Jackson named a branch of their library after Wright, though black people had been barred from using the facility when he lived there.

Wright's childhood in Mississippi was a miserable one. The constant anxiety and complexity of navigating race relations was compounded by the transience of his living situation and a household run by a strict Adventist grandmother, who often viciously beat him. In 1945,

Wright published his autobiography, *Black Boy*, detailing the difficulties of his childhood before he moved from Jackson to Memphis and, finally, on to Chicago. (The original manuscript included a second part about his years in Chicago; this section was published posthumously under the title *American Hunger*.)

Native Son is usually presented as the entry point to Wright's work, the obvious high school reading-list choice. A story illustrating the suffocation of segregation, *Native Son* is a brave book, one of the first novels to describe exactly how disastrous the regime of American racism has been for its citizens. As Irving Howe observed in *Dissent*, "Richard Wright's novel brought out into the open, as no one ever had before, the hatred, fear and violence that have crippled and may yet destroy our culture. A blow at the white man, the novel forced him to recognize himself as an oppressor. A blow at the black man, the novel forced him to recognize the cost of his submission."

But *Black Boy*, a book so vivid and unflinching that it is occasionally painful to read, is the Wright book that hooked me. It is a coming-of-age tale where the happy ending—Wright becomes a bestselling author living in Europe—seems impossible. Wright describes a society that has been systematically and thoroughly rigged against him, the unending struggle to nourish himself in the face of people set on his starvation. Robert Park, the sociologist and colleague of Booker T. Washington, once famously greeted Wright with the question, "How in hell did you happen?" *Black Boy* is Wright's answer, and it's an incredible one.

Wright's life didn't begin in Jackson, and neither does *Black Boy*. It opens in Natchez, Mississippi, where Wright lived with his grandparents and mother as a small child. The opening pages of the book are Wright's account of a time when, as a bored four-year-old with instructions not to bother his sick grandmother, he fed straw from a broom into the fireplace and accidentally set the house ablaze. That house, improbably, is still standing and bears the historic marker that the patch of earth in Jackson lacks. I decided to follow the trail that Wright sets out in *Black Boy*, from Natchez back up to Jackson, to see what traces of his life remained there.

Natchez is about two hours south of Jackson, a pleasant meander down the Natchez Trace Parkway, a winding road laid down on old sections of a trail originally cut through the Mississippi woods by Native Americans. It's a route that's slower and less direct than the interstate, but it makes up in scenery what it lacks in efficiency. On the way down, I spotted a pickup truck with its bed crammed full of sweet potatoes, as well as several crews of motorcyclists, who favor the parkway for its lower speed limit, ban on commercial traffic, and lack of stop signs. Along the road are the remnants of Rocky Springs, an abandoned Civil War town where picnickers stop to eat sandwiches amid the ruins. Not too far from the Trace, just past the town of Port Gibson, are the Windsor Ruins, the moss-encrusted columns of a Greek-style antebellum mansion that burned to the ground in 1890. The Trace lures a certain breed of Southern ghost hunters and romantics; it's a trail where the history of the state seems much closer than the endless rows of Walmarts and gas stations that dot the interstate. As I wound off the Trace toward the town, I took a detour to the junction of US Routes 84 and 61 North, where, in 2008, the state put up a marker to designate a section of the road "Richard Wright Memorial Highway." The blue sign flashed in the sunlight as I drove past.

Wright was born on the Rucker Plantation in Adams County, an area that has now been almost entirely consumed by the Natchez State Park. His grandparents had all been slaves, brought through Natchez when the town was at the center of the Southern slave trade. Wright's ancestors are scattered around Adams County. Wright's second cousin, Charles Wright, is still a Natchez resident, and at the annual Natchez Literary and Cinema Celebration, he leads a Richard Wright ramble—a tour of the physical places where Wright and his Mississippi relatives once lived. One of the stops on the tour is Forks of the Road, the slave market just outside of Natchez, where Nathaniel Wright, Richard's grandfather, arrived from Virginia to be sold.

At the time that Wright's ancestors were forcibly relocated to Mississippi, Natchez was a teeming port city, stuffed with wealthy planters and businessmen making the most of its location on the edge of the Mississippi River. Originally a French settlement, Natchez was the original capital of the state and its first economic center. Plantation owners loaded cotton onto steamships in Natchez for distribution downriver in New Orleans. Forks of the Road became a nexus for the Southern slave trade, funneling men and women from the Upper South to farms and plantations in Mississippi. From 1830 until 1863, when Abraham Lincoln signed the Emancipation Proclamation, tens of thousands of black men and women were bought and sold there, including Wright's grandfather, Nathaniel. After the Union Army took control of Vicksburg, Nathaniel Wright volunteered to serve as part of the troops occupying Natchez.

Forks of the Road is now a series of sun-bleached informational plaques across from a strip mall filled with auto-repair shops and barbecue restaurants. The slave trade had been banned from the city proper in the 1830s for fear of cholera, so traders set up their human wares just outside the boundaries of Natchez. The plaques, in the matter-of-fact language of historical markers, explain the stomach-churning cruelty of the slave trade, the oldest and deepest American wound: children separated from their parents, men and women taken against their will, vicious and ongoing abuse from plantation owners. Forks of the Road was more of a showroom than an auction house; buyers would inspect the pool of people and select one or more for purchase. Where those showrooms stood is now a thick line of trees. One of the placards listed the Union troops who had helped forcibly end operations of the slave trade at Forks of the Road. Nathaniel Wright's name was on the list.

Richard Wright's maternal grandfather, Richard Wilson, also fought for the Union Army, though he never received his promised disability payment from the government. Wright describes Wilson in *Black Boy* as a man with a quick temper who harbored lingering resentment against the shoddy treatment he received from the War Department. Wilson kept his Army gun loaded in the corner of his room, on the off chance that the War Between the States might resume. Wright also describes Wilson's daily visits to the mailbox in hopes that the government would make good on their pension promise, and his grandparents' ongoing bitterness over yet another mistreatment from white people in charge. "I never heard him speak of white people; I think he hated them too much to talk of them," Wright wrote.

Downtown Natchez is a place that screams "quaint" from every cornice. Old plantation homes wrap around a downtown crammed with antique stores and cafés and ritzy hotels. Riverboat casinos float along the Mississippi River. But outside the blocks downtown, it's clear that Natchez is a tattered town, mended in strategic places. The house where Wright lived is in the historic black neighborhood of Woodlawn. Scattered among the well-tended homes on his block are houses with plywood nailed over the windows and rotting screen porches. The place where Wright lived with his maternal grandparents, the one that he accidentally set fire to, is painted an upbeat bright yellow. I counted five sets of wind chimes on the porch, alongside a multicolored miniature hot-air balloon, put in place for the town's annual River Balloon Race.

Wright's childhood memories of the house are full of mixed emotions. His grandmother was quick with the lash, once beating Wright so badly that he lost consciousness. But Wright also details, in *Black Boy*, scenes of beauty, of "the vague sense of the infinite as I looked down upon the yellow, dreaming waters of the Mississippi River" and "vast hazes of gold washed earthward from star-heavy skies on silent nights."

Before I left Natchez, I walked downtown to the Museum of African American History and Culture, where I met David Dreyer, a historian who had helped Charles Wright lead his ramble and who had helped curate the museum's wall of Wright-related memorabilia. The museum has copies of Wright's books and a replica of the typewriter he favored, but, unsurprisingly, there isn't much in the way of artifacts. At the museum, Dreyer sat down and flipped through a binder of documents related to Wright's time in Natchez, including a photo of Wright's daughter, Julia, who had flown from Paris to unveil the highway marker. Dreyer was part of a group of local historians and Wright academics who had pushed for the establishment of the sign. His work at the museum is a counterpoint to the tourist industry that presents a whitewashed version of Natchez's past, the romantic vision of proper gentlemen and Southern belles sipping iced tea in their spacious homes. In 2009, Dreyer wrote an editorial in the *Natchez Democrat* protesting the town's motto, "Where the Old South Still Lives," as one that glorified the town's racist past. "It may seem like an insignificant difference, but if you had told me that Natchez was 'the cradle of Mississippi,' rather than a place where slavery and Jim Crow were still honored, I might have discovered the secret sooner and moved here ten years earlier," he wrote.

Embracing Richard Wright is part of the museum's mission to present the history of the region without glorifying the trappings of slavery. Dreyer showed me a map of the world, on which he had tracked Wright's travels, from Mississippi to the Northeast and beyond, then later travels to Senegal, Japan, and India. There's a picture on the wall of a Wright family reunion where Wright's father had been in attendance. As best as scholars can figure out, Wright had returned to Natchez just once after the beginning of his successful writing career. "He gave his father, who was a sharecropper, a set of false teeth," Dreyer said. "But his dad didn't have much use for them, so, the story goes, he hung the teeth in a tree in his backyard."

From Natchez, Richard Wright's family had moved to Memphis. But his time there was brief and full of tragedy. His father left the family and took up with another woman, leaving Wright's mother to try to find enough work to support her two children. Wright, left to his own devices, began sneaking into Memphis saloons to beg drinks off strangers and tussle with street gangs. Wright's mother was barely making ends meet. "Hunger had always been more or less at my elbow when I played, but now I began to wake up at night to find hunger standing at my bedside, staring at me gauntly," Wright wrote. Eventually, his mother temporarily placed Wright and his brother in an orphanage until the family moved away, back to Mississippi.

But Memphis, years later, also became the place where Wright began reading the novels that would fuel his writing career. After Wright finished middle school, he saved up to move North; Memphis was his first stop. He found work at an optical company there, and, one day on the job in 1925, spotted an article in the Memphis *Commercial Appeal* lambasting an article by the critic and essayist H. L. Mencken. Wright's curiosity was immediately piqued: "Were there, then, people other than Negroes who criticized the South?" he wondered. Wright, determined to find out more about Mencken, hit upon a strategy to circumnavigate the segregated public-library rules that prevented him from checking out books. He found a sympathetic white Irish Catholic coworker (referred to in *Black Boy* as Mr. Falk) who loaned Wright his library card. With the help of the card and some forged notes to the librarian, Wright suddenly had access to all manner of riches. He checked out Mencken's *Prejudices* and *A Book of Prefaces*, and was quickly enraptured by Mencken's prose and strong opinions. "I was jarred and shocked by the style, the clear, clean sweeping sentences," Wright notes in *Black Boy*. "He was using words as a weapon, using them as one would use a club."

Mencken, an outspoken critic of the cloistered culture of the post–Civil War South, is a pivotal figure in Southern literature thanks in part to his blistering essay "The Sahara of the Bozart," published in 1917, in which Mencken decried "that gargantuan paradise of the fourth-rate" below the Mason-Dixon line. "In the North, of course, there is also grossness, crassness, vulgarity. The North, in its way, is also stupid and obnoxious," Mencken wrote. "But nowhere in the North is there such complete sterility, so depressing a lack of all civilized gesture and aspiration." Wright was not the only Southern writer who was motivated by Mencken's indictment; many novelists, such as Eudora Welty and Flannery O'Connor, wrote in opposition to Mencken's statements. But Wright is unique in seeing Mencken's writings not as a challenge but as a foothold. Wright looked up the names of writers whom Mencken mentioned, and soon began devouring books. Thanks to the library card, Wright's perspective on his life in Memphis began to shift. Reading Sinclair Lewis's *Main Street*, Wright wrote, made him see his boss as a particular type, one that closely resembled Lewis's conformist middle-class protagonist George F. Babbitt.

Wright began sneaking books into work wrapped in newspaper, and his reading confirmed his own experiences of discrimination in the South, strengthening his resolve to leave. "I no longer *felt* that the world about me was hostile, killing; I *knew* it," he wrote. The place that fueled these revelations, Cossitt Library, still stands today in Memphis, just on the edge of the Mississippi River, though a 1958 renovation has dramatically altered its appearance since Wright's days there. (Because of its association with Wright, the library became Tennessee's first literary landmark registered with the American Library Association.) It's not too far from Beale Street, the famous thoroughfare where Wright lived in a room with a woman named Mrs. Moss. Beale Street, once an ill-reputed area full of after-hours clubs, jazz venues, and brothels, is now Memphis's main tourist drag, a mixture of Times Square and Bourbon Street with a busker-provided saxophone soundtrack. But even now, visiting Memphis, you can imagine it: a wide-eyed Wright, fresh off the train from Jackson, taking in the crowds and the music, a copy of *Sister Carrie* wrapped in newsprint under his arm as he wandered home.

AFTER THEY LEFT NATCHEZ, Wright's family moved several more times, including a brief stay in Elaine, Arkansas, where Wright had one of his first serious brushes with the harsh logic of racism. A group of white men murdered Wright's uncle Hoskins in order to take over his blossoming liquor business, and his mother and aunt were forced to flee town without attending to his funeral or claiming any of his assets.

This was as close as white terror had ever come to me and my mind reeled. Why had we not fought back, I asked my mother, and the fear that was in her made her slap me into silence.

It is scenes in *Black Boy* like this one where Wright makes plain the awful weight of the Jim Crow South, the nameless and omnipresent fear that it fostered. Wright's mother and grandmother were strict disciplinarians; they did not hesitate to use the lash when Wright broke their rules. But what's made hauntingly clear, as Wright looks at his childhood from the vantage point of an outwardly successful adulthood, is that this was an inherited kind of violence. Those whippings were a crude kind of protection: As much as Wright suffered at the hands of his mother and grandparents, it was nothing compared to the anguish that a white man could inflict suddenly for the tiniest, most mysterious violation of a largely unspoken social order. These hard lessons were intended to save Wright's life. Talking back to his grandmother would earn him a sound beating, but talking back to a white man, as Wright learned, could result in his death. Even though Wright rebels against the rules at home, he recognizes that they were a way of teaching the brutal truth of what it meant to grow up black in the South in the 1910s and 1920s. This was the structure of Wright's childhood, the cycle of violence perpetuated by white Southerners. In *Black Boy*, again and again, Wright faces down the menacing senselessness of racism. After the incident in Arkansas, he writes, a dread of white people was cemented in his mind. "I had already grown to feel that there existed men against whom I was powerless, men who could violate my life at will." This was what struck me when I first read *Black Boy* as a white woman growing up in a South where the icons of the civil rights movement had been turned into statues and museum exhibits while the legacy of disenfranchisement persisted. Wright's writing presents the racism for what it is: not a hidden, intangible facet of society, not something that is inevitably going to end, but a constant, shifting horror, as inescapable as the weather.

Wright moved to Jackson again after his mother suffered a paralytic stroke, forcing the family to separate him from his brother and place them in separate family households. What followed was the only unbroken stretch of schooling that Wright managed to attain, at the Smith Robertson School in Jackson, a time that sparked his curiosity in the written word, though did not exactly nourish his ambitions. His grandmother's devotion to her church is a constant sticking point in *Black Boy*. Wright hears his first novel read aloud, *Bluebeard and His Seven Wives*, courtesy of a woman named Ella, a boarder in his grandmother's house. "The tale made the world around me throb, live," Wright writes. But Wright's grandmother catches the two mid-reading and informs Wright that fiction is "the Devil's work," and ultimately evicts Ella. Wright was hooked, though he could not afford to begin to read seriously until he left Jackson for good.

In his grandmother's household, Wright rebelled against her Seventh-Day Adventist fervor. The reasons he gives in *Black Boy* are simple: He wanted to work on Saturday, the Adventist Sabbath, in order to earn enough for more than his standard meals of greens and gravy, which barely sustained him. His grandmother's promises of hellfire and hope for his salvation did not impress Wright as much as the more urgent concerns of his everyday life. Though he was eventually baptized as Methodist to please his mother, Wright maintained a deep suspicion of religion as a tool for the oppression of black people in the South. As he explained in one lecture,

> I lived my childhood under a racial code, bru-
> tal and bloody, that white men proclaimed was
> ordained of God, said was mandatory by nature
> of their religion. Naturally, I rejected that reli-
> gion and would reject any religion which pre-
> scribes for me an inferior position in life; I reject
> that tradition and any tradition which proscribes
> my humanity.

But Wright's rejection of his grandmother's faith made growing up even more difficult. His stance against the Church meant that Wright found himself alienated from most of his family, a lost cause inside his own home.

Smith Robertson Junior High School in downtown Jackson is one of the few architectural remnants of Wright's childhood that remains, the place where he had most of his formal education. It was my first stop on the way back from Natchez, driving back from the wooded Trace into the familiar traffic of downtown Jackson. Wright used to walk the mile and a half to Smith Robertson and back until he obtained a bicycle. During his time there, the school had been a simple brick building, but in 1929, the school had gotten an Art Deco facelift from a local architectural firm. I parked in front of the locked gate and peered inside. The white cement façade is a remnant from a time of a different Jackson, one where the downtown did not empty back into the suburbs every night. The school is now a museum dedicated to Jackson's African American heritage, though it seemed a forbidding place to potential visitors.

Inside that school building is where Wright made his first steps toward a writing career. While attending Smith Robertson, Wright had written his first short story, "The Voodoo of Hell's Half-Acre," and published it in the black weekly newspaper the *Southern Register.* This first literary triumph was met with suspicion from his friends and admonishment from his grandmother for using the word "hell." No copy of it remains. When Wright graduated from Smith Robertson, he was named valedictorian of his class. But the honor led to another clash with authority. Wright refused to give a speech that the principal had written for his graduation, drawing up his own instead. Despite pressure from his classmates and teachers, Wright delivered his own speech. "I did not care if they liked it or not; I was through," he writes.

Not far from the school is Farish Street, Jackson's historic black district. After Wright graduated from middle school, Wright threw himself into working in order to earn enough money to relocate from Jackson. One of his gigs was as a ticket taker in a theater on Farish Street, then a busy shopping district and nighttime hub. Now, as I walked down the street where Wright used to work, the district was largely empty, caught in a legal battle between the city and developers who hoped to revive the area. Construction of some of the storefronts had stopped abruptly, their glinting windows empty, the insides still full of stacked plywood. Some of the buildings' roofs had long ago collapsed in, the walls reclaimed by vines. Only three storefronts gave a hint of the Farish Street that was around when Wright lived here: a shoe-repair store, the Jackson Police Museum, and the Big Apple Inn, a diner famous for its tamales and pig-ear sandwiches. Medgar Evers used to have an office above the space. Today, part of the structure looks on the verge of collapse.

While I was walking among the ruins of Farish Street, I thought about Welty's house, preserved right down to the knickknacks, the care and expertise that had been put into her legacy, and the sharp contrast between

Welty's visitor center and the grassy patch of unmarked earth where Wright's house once stood and the abandoned storefronts on Farish Street. I thought about the logic behind destroying one landmark and pouring funds into another; the slow, almost grudging acknowledgment of Wright's brilliance; the library named for him in Jackson that he could not have entered without fear of violence. Alice Walker, who grew up near Flannery O'Connor in Georgia, wrote an essay about her visit to O'Connor's abandoned house: "What I feel at the moment of knocking is fury that someone is paid to take care of her house, though no one lives in it, and that hers, in fact stands, while mine—which of course we never owned anyway—Is slowly rotting into dust." Walker wrote, "I think: it all comes back to houses. . . . I think: I would level this country with the sweep of my hand if I could." And I wondered: If Wright had not died in 1960, if he had returned to Jackson from his life in Paris as a world-famous novelist, if he had somehow visited the Welty house and wandered down to Farish Street, would he, too, be stunned by the injustice of it all? Would he think *it all comes back to houses*? Or would he walk through the streets knowing that, physical evidence or no, he had left a mark on this place?

Wright survived the punishments meted out to him by his white employers and finally accumulated enough money to move to Memphis, where his mother would later join him. On my way out of downtown Jackson I stopped at the train station, just south of Farish Street, where I imagined Wright making his escape, finally beginning his lifelong self-extrication process from the Jim Crow South. But the South, even as he built his new life and rocketed to success, continued to haunt Wright. In the original ending of *Black Boy*, one excised when the book was posthumously expanded to include his later memoirs, Wright speeds away to the hope of the North.

> I was not leaving the South to forget the South . . .
> In leaving, I was taking a part of the South to transplant in alien soil, to see if it could grow differently, if it could drink of new and cool rains, bend in strange winds, respond to the warmth of other suns, and perhaps, to bloom. . . . And if that miracle ever happened, then I would know that there was yet hope in that southern swamp of despair and violence, that light could emerge even out of the blackest of the southern night.

The South that Wright imagined, a place that can accept and celebrate, whatever their race, all its native children, hasn't come to pass—not yet. The burden remains, as does the fear and the legacy of violence. But into that Southern swamp, Wright's work shone a light.

3. William Faulkner's Liquor Cabinet
OXFORD, MS

Roughly two and a half hours to the northeast of Jackson, just short of the Tennessee line, is the location of the most famous literary tourist destination in the Deep South: the former residence of William Faulkner in Oxford, Mississippi. Faulkner and Wright never met, to my knowledge, but were mutual admirers. When Black Boy *came out in 1940, Faulkner sent a letter to Wright commending him for expressing "what needed to be said" about race relations in America. Welty and Faulkner were friends; in 1943 he struck up a correspondence by sending a postcard praising* The Robber Bridegroom, *opening with, "Dear Welty: You are doing fine. You are doing all right." The two met on several occasions, once going on a sailboat ride together, but Welty found his literary influence hard to shake. She described writing in Mississippi while Faulkner was alive to "living near a big mountain, something majestic. Its magnitude, all by itself, made it something remote."*

PEOPLE IN OXFORD love to talk about William Faulkner. Accounts of what Billy Faulkner was *really* like are as frequently swapped as tales from Elvis's coterie. Faulkner is their most famous resident and juiciest piece of gossip, the man whose home draws hundreds of visitors to the county seat every year and the one whose novels painted an indelible, vivid, and often damning portrait of their town. Some fifty years after his death, Faulkner is more a part of the social atmosphere of Oxford than he ever was in his life, the subject of festivals, writing contests, drinking contests, legend, and lore. The marvelous local independent bookstore, Square Books, has an entire section devoted to Faulkner and Faulkner studies. Rowan Oak, the home Faulkner lived in for most of his life, is the treasure of the University of Mississippi's holdings. The twenty-nine acres surrounding Rowan Oak are laced with hiking trails and dotted with picnic spots.

On any given visit to the grounds, you're likely to find a half dozen sorority sisters jogging, a smattering of aspiring artists sketching the columns of the antebellum house, and one or two bored-looking lit students on work-study ushering people in for a self-guided tour. Before football games, professors and Oxfordians gather in front of Rowan Oak to grill burgers and drink beer. At Faulkner's grave, in St. Peter's Cemetery, you can find bottles of bourbon in various states of emptiness alongside crumpled cans of Bud Light, evidence of tributes by English-worshipping Ole Miss students turned into full-scale revelry. Faulkner is as much a university mascot as Colonel Reb, the wizened Confederate gentleman that led the Ole Miss football team to occasional glory until being replaced in 2010 by the less controversial "Rebel Black Bear," which was itself named for Faulkner's short story "The Bear."

Faulkner has become a fixture, not just in Oxford but throughout the whole state. In 2005, an advertising agency seeking to combat Mississippi's negative image delivered posters to every public school and airport that featured Faulkner's face, along with the claim, "Yeah, we can read. A few of us can even write." In a state that regularly ranks at the bottom in public-health and education surveys, Faulkner is the conversational counterpoint, the rebuff to Mississippi bashers.

But in Oxford, Faulkner is more than the mythical figure that brought home Mississippi's first Nobel Prize for Literature. His legend is something like that of a bum uncle who died and revealed a hidden fortune— the very kind of uncle Southerners love to talk about. He was a college dropout with a tendency to exaggerate his experience as a veteran of World War I. Though he had been enrolled in the RAF, Faulkner never saw combat. He would walk around town in a uniform he had bought from a pawnshop, feigning a limp. Faulkner was a D student in high school, and also notoriously awful at the jobs he held in Oxford before his writing career took off. He was a lackluster handyman, fixing boilers or hanging wallpaper for a few dollars, earning the local title of "Count No Account," or more often, just "Count No 'Count." His family considered him eccentric at best and a total embarrassment at worst. When asked about his nephew, Faulkner's own uncle, John Wesley Thompson Falkner II (the family name originally was spelled without the "u," but William Faulkner changed his in 1918 when he joined the Canadian Royal Air Force), famously complained, "There's a black sheep in every family and Billy's ours. Not worth a cent."

As the university postmaster, Faulkner was particularly atrocious. He would hide in the back, playing bridge with his friends and tinkering with his stories. He would often forget to deliver envelopes or leaf through magazines before giving them to their recipients. His October 1924 resignation letter is famously unrepentant and widely quoted: "As long as I live under the capitalistic system, I expect to have my life influenced by the demands of moneyed people," Faulkner wrote. "But I will be damned if I propose to be at the beck and call of every itinerant scoundrel who has two cents to invest in a postage stamp." (This did not, however, prevent the postal system from issuing a commemorative stamp in Faulkner's likeness in 1987.) The town square's department store, Neilson's, still has a framed letter from Faulkner reneging on his debts, inviting them to "Sue and be damned. . . . You may even get an autographed book. That will be worth a damn sight more than my autograph on a check dated ten months from now"—a boast that turned out to be mostly accurate. Faulkner was even fired from a two-year turn as the Scoutmaster of a local Boy Scout troop on account of his drinking.

Faulkner's love of a good stiff drink is one of the grand parts of his legend. The two things that always stood out most to me about Faulkner's home are the bookshelves—custom made to store his shotgun shells along the sides—and the impressive array of empty bottles in Faulkner's old liquor cabinet. Sitting next to his well-used silver julep cup, there's an assortment of whiskeys, featuring his favorite, Four Roses. There's a heavy-looking bottle of Harvey's Fine Tawny Hunting Port, which Faulkner preferred for cooking game birds. There's a bottle of French wine, which Faulkner developed a taste for after winning the Nobel Prize. Tucked in beside the bottles is a copy of Faulkner's mint julep recipe.

On later trips to Rowan Oak, I would always sojourn upstairs to see the cabinet, stare at the faded labels and colored glass. The liquor cabinet is one of the few remaining hints of the messiness of Faulkner's life. The papers have been whisked away to archives, the pipes and watches kept as heirlooms by family members, the knickknacks filed away at museums. Aside from the scrawled-out plot of *A Fable* on the walls of the downstairs bedroom—"Monday: The French regiment mutinies, refuses to leave the trench to make an attack, is drawn out, disarmed, put under arrest and sent to the rear"—and an envelope from the Famous Writers School addressed to Faulkner at the "Humdrum Mansion," a practical joke from his family, the cabinet feels like the closest remains of Faulkner's true spirit—that of a flawed, fragile, and brilliant person. The empty bottles are talismans, some of the few physical possessions of Faulkner's that seem to connect him to his experience as a writer.

"Civilization begins with distillation," he once said—now a favorite line among cocktail aficionados and frat boys alike. His fondness for alcohol confirms just how much he believed in his own theory. "Brother Will drank what was cheap and available," his nephew Jimmy recounted. In his then-dry county, this included both gin and tonics on the porch and 200-proof corn whiskey out on the field, sitting outside with his brother and his childhood pet snake, Penelope. One of the most prominent figures in Oxford while Faulkner lived there was Motee Daniels, the local bootlegger, who later ran for coroner and county ranger, with his dog, Buster, as his campaign manager. Faulkner would have crates of white lightning delivered by train to his door. "The tools I need for my trade are paper, tobacco, food, and a little whiskey," the author remarked to *The Paris Review* in 1956. When the interviewer, Jean Stein, asked if he meant bourbon, Faulkner countered, "I ain't that particular. Between Scotch and nothing, I'll take Scotch."

His drunken benders are a lot of mythology and addiction-counseling warnings. Any remembrance of the man almost always includes a yarn about some truly dedicated partying. In Hollywood, Faulkner, upon meeting producer Nunnally Johnson, cut his hand on a pint of whiskey and held aloft his injured finger, dripping blood into his hat while he guzzled down the bottle. The two were found in an Okie camp three weeks later, just after a binge of Brobdingnagian proportions. After completing *The Sound and The Fury*, Faulkner locked himself in his room and drank until he blacked out. He burned himself badly on a steam pipe in a New York City hotel, too far gone to notice the scalding heat as he passed out on the fixture. In Oxford, Faulkner once arrived home from a night out wearing the hat of the town drunk, Charlie. The two had apparently swapped clothes on a lark.

During the restoration on his home at Rowan Oak the construction workers supposedly found his bedroom ceiling full of holes made by Faulkner flinging bottles through the ceiling. When they inspected the attic, the floor was covered in broken glass, a pile of Four Roses whiskey bottles in disarray in the corner. Though Faulkner was far from the first author to have a complicated relationship with drinking, his antics solidified the portrait of a Southern Renaissance author, a man as handy with a rifle as he was with a typewriter—a hard-drinking, hard-living, rowdy sophisticate.

But Faulkner was more than a drunk with writing talent. He secretly set up a local food pantry, administered out of the general store. After his first child, Alabama, died a few days after her birth, Faulkner made sure every local hospital had an incubator to care for premature children. His daughter, Jill, and youngest niece, Dean, called him "Pappy" and remember fondly his elaborate ritual of serving them hot toddies when they were ill. Dean Faulkner Wells's remembrances are the warmer side of Faulkner's legacy, the campfires and cotillions and Christmases. Wells took over the restoration of Rowan Oak, kept the writing desk on which Faulkner wrote *Absalom, Absalom!*, and later lent it to Jimmy Buffett to complete his own novel. She was the one who decided which portraits of Faulkner's mother to keep on the walls, which of his books to display, and how the grounds should be kept. Until her death in 2011, Wells kept a small salon of literary fellows, entertaining writers and interested parties passing through. She also judged the annual "faux Faulkner" contest, where mimics would do their best bad Faulkner impression. And it was Wells who decided to keep the liquor cabinet out, as a tribute to Pappy and a reminder of his spirit and vulnerability. Faulkner's recklessness and his intelligence, his gentility and cruelty, became symbolic not just of the Southern literary scene but also of the region itself, a place made of delicacy and brutality in equal parts.

FAULKNER WAS A PRODUCT of the local culture of Oxford, a tightly knit community where churchgoing patricians could be discovered in backroom juke joints the night before services. Oxford's six-term former mayor, John Leslie, was also the town pharmacist. Oxfordians often pulled pranks on the good-natured Leslie, calling in fake town emergencies to get the mayor out of bed in the wee hours. Faulkner's Oxford was the place where women ran Bible studies out of their general store, where the way to counter the venom of a copperhead bite was to keep the affected limb raised above your head, and the tatters of antebellum politesse still reigned. The complex fictional galaxy of Faulkner's Yoknapatawpha County is all based on his sleepy hometown. This is why Faulkner decided to return to Oxford from New York and New Orleans. As he told *The Paris Review*:

> Beginning with *Sartoris* I discovered that my own little postage stamp of native soil was worth writing about and that I would never live long enough to exhaust it, and that by sublimating the actual into the apocryphal I would have complete liberty to use whatever talent I might have to its absolute top. It opened up a gold mine of other people, so I created a cosmos of my own.

Yoknapatawpha was that cosmos, the place where Faulkner could fully explore the grace and gallantries of his South.

Anyone searching for a clue to which places provided Faulkner with specific models for his fiction need look no further than the framed drawing of the county and family territories that hangs on the wall of Rowan Oak, or the map that the author sketched of Yoknapatawpha and published at the end of *Absalom, Absalom!* The university has a pamphlet for a whole driving tour, eagerly followed by the Faulkner scholars and literary pilgrims who pile into Oxford for the annual Faulkner conference. The author's legacy attracts an average of 25,000 visitors every year. Scholars shuttle from corner to corner of Oxford's Lafayette County, hunting for hints.

Sally Wolff-King, a professor of Southern studies at Emory University, has spent much of her life connecting the dots between Faulkner's stream-of-consciousness work and actual places. She's a particular expert on a Civil War–era plantation diary found in 2010, the volume from which she believes Faulkner sourced many of the names of his characters. Wolff-King conducts annual Faulkner tours for her eager undergraduates, ferrying them to many of the locations she believes Faulkner used in his books. There's the Thompson-Chandler house, a sturdy, solemn Greek revival house on South Thirteenth Street that served as the inspiration for the bedraggled patrician mansion of the Compson family in *The Sound and the Fury*. There's the lyrically named Shadowlawn, a quiet, unassuming house Wolff-King and other Faulknerites think was the site for Faulkner's creepy short story masterpiece "A Rose For Emily." In the town square, there's the courthouse, with the statue of a Confederate soldier Faulkner wrote about in *The Sound and the Fury*, who "gazed with empty eyes beneath his marble hand in wind and weather." (A bronze plaque in the square reminds Faulkner readers of the passage, for those who can't so readily draw up the quote.) Meg Faulkner Duchaine, Faulkner's grandniece, still lives on the edge of town, and gives tours of her Pappy's pipe and treasured first editions on request.

What are we searching for in Oxford, amid the Yazoo clay? There is something about Faulkner's work that stirs the souls of Southerners, something that reads deeply and essentially true. "The deep South," Faulkner wrote in *Absalom, Absalom!*, "dead since 1865 and peopled with garrulous outraged baffled ghosts." To be Southern is to grow up among the ruins. Southernness suggests a deep, inescapable past, an inability to move forward without the weight of your ancestors. Faulkner's modernist prose and tangled chronological structures seemed to encompass it aptly. There is a deep emotional conflict at the heart of his work and at the heart of the town of Oxford itself. Mississippi is the land of debutantes and lynching, a defeated country, stuck and reveling in its own stagnancy. It engenders a feeling to which any traveler to Deep South from above the Mason-Dixon can relate: that wish to simultaneously defend and renounce your home.

Faulkner's work is always coming back to this paradox. His little postage stamp of soil horrified him as much as it intrigued him. After the death of Emmett Till, he wrote a long essay despairing of his native Mississippians. "To live anywhere in the world today and be against equality because of race or color, is like living in Alaska and being against snow," he wrote in *Harper's*. "We have already got snow." At home, Faulkner faced sneers from his contemporaries. In the press, critics lambasted him for not explicitly attacking Jim Crow laws in his fiction. Faulkner kept a low profile, but he surely felt exasperated and disappointed. "Home again, his native land," Faulkner wrote in an essay on Mississippi for *Holiday*. "He was born of it and his bones will sleep in it; loving it even while hating some of it."

I grew up understanding the intricacies of social courtesies and children's calling cards, knowing the difference between good and bad cheese grits. But there was also the ever-present hum of guilt, the knowledge of living on the site of injustice. When I first read *The Sound and the Fury*, it struck me as a breathtaking account of the paradoxes of the region. That was what it meant to be Southern, to be obsessed and repulsed by the past, to not be able to get over things. Faulkner's writing became all mixed up in the beauty and tragedy of Mississippi, appearing effusive, jumbled, glorious, threatening to spill over the page at any moment. Eudora Welty wrote of one Faulkner sentence that it "races like a dinosaur across the early fields of time. It runs along with the quality of seeming to happen all at once." That's exactly it: Faulkner's work almost seems like a natural occurrence, an amazing aberration that only the contrivances of nature could produce.

When I visited Oxford the first time, it seemed to me a sacred place. The scenery wove into the collective memory of literature. The grounds of Rowan Oak seemed to me filled with the spirits of Dilsey and Quentin, Caddie's muddied britches flapping on the line.

Benjy's synesthetic raptures came back to me in pieces. The treacherous Snopes family seemed to be lurking around the bend; I wouldn't have been entirely surprised if a bearded, bayonet-bearing soldier had come stumbling into the backyard. The vividness of Faulkner's writing almost made the place itself seem duller, less sharply outlined. It speaks to Faulkner's skill that the world he made was so alive that people like to speak of it like history and genealogy instead of fiction. His characters don't seem fictional so much as far-off.

I'm not sure exactly what I wanted from Rowan Oak—perhaps the soothing gaudiness of Graceland, a gift shop or a quiz where you could find out which Faulkner character was most like your personality. But really, like everyone who visits, I wanted a piece of the man himself, to hold an object that he had touched in the hopes that it would transfer some of his talent. I supposed myself a student of literature, and Faulkner was my tutor. As a young writer, I wrote long, exuberantly terrible poems that I imagined to be in his style. I devoured his books at a rapid pace. Some tattered, half-understood Faulkner tome was always in the back of my car, underlined to near extinction.

The drama of Yoknapatawpha influenced my slowly forming sense of myself, not just as a writer but also as a Southerner, and a sometimes queasy, sometimes proud inheritor of all that the South entailed. I made my own kind of mental shrine to him. I even made a makeshift medal, a silver locket containing a piece of a page from a disintegrated copy of *The Sound and the Fury* that had one of my favorite lines, one that seemed to describe exactly the treachery of Southerners' obsession with time: "That Christ was not crucified: he was worn away by a minute clicking of little wheels."

Even as he described the world of rural farmers, African American nannies, soldiers, and spoiled children, he was creating an identity. Southern literature wasn't much of a category before Faulkner. His writing, and success, spurred a generation of writers from Alabama, Georgia, Mississippi, and Tennessee to take up their pens and mine their own territory.

That is why I came to Oxford. It's why thousands of visitors file through every year, literature students still drink to the memory of a man their parents are too young to remember, and turn in theses on Faulkner's writing and race or agriculture or feminism. To be able to sketch even the most vague outlines of the complications of the human experience is a rare and valuable thing. It's why anyone writes, in the hope to communicate not just what was there but what it was like, why it mattered. Faulkner did that, and he did it by concentrating on his postage stamp of dirt. Faulkner created his own cosmos, and then Oxford became it.

4. Flannery O'Connor's Peacocks
MILLEDGEVILLE, GA

Milledgeville is about 430 miles to the east of Oxford, across Alabama entirely and into the center of Georgia. Like Eudora Welty, Flannery O'Connor made sure to mark out a distance from William Faulkner's work, though she admired his writing greatly. "I keep clear of Faulkner so my own little boat won't get swamped," she wrote to a friend. Confined to her family farm, Andalusia, by illness, O'Connor worked on her own fictional landscape, one where the burden was religious rather than historical, and the clotted imagery of small-town Southern life gave way to menacing preachers, surly shut-ins, and possessed petty criminals.

FLANNERY O'CONNOR LIVED her short life surrounded by birds. Her fascination with the creatures began as a child, when she was growing up under the shadow of the Cathedral of Saint John the Baptist in a narrow house on Lafayette Square in the Irish section of Savannah, Georgia. Her mother allowed O'Connor chickens as a substitute for a dog or cat, and the little girl kept them on the back porch of her home. At five years old, O'Connor attracted the attention of

Pathé, a British newsreel company, after teaching her pet Cochin bantam hen to walk backwards. The short, scratchy video, titled "Do You Reverse?" shows a young O'Connor, then still going by her given name, Mary, struggling to hold on to the little chicken as it flutters, alarmed, at her shoulder.

"From that day with the Pathé man I began to collect chickens," O'Connor wrote in "Living with a Peacock," an essay for *Holiday* magazine later retitled "The King of the Birds." "What had been only a mild interest became a passion, a quest. I had to have more and more chickens." As a child, O'Connor sought out birds with odd characteristics, like different-colored eyes or crooked combs. She sewed tiny, proper outfits for her pets. "A gray bantam named Colonel Eggbert wore a white pique coat with a lace collar and two buttons in the back," O'Connor wrote. She named her pets after historical figures, family members, and friends. She named a rooster Haile Selassie, kept a quail dubbed Amelia Earhart, and insisted on bringing a chicken named Aloysius, resplendent in a jacket and bow tie, to her Girl Scout meetings. In order to pass her home economics course at Peabody High School, O'Connor sewed an entire wardrobe of clothes to fit a duckling.

O'Connor's childhood home in Savannah is now a visitor site. She lived there with her mother, Regina, and father, Edward, in Savannah for her first thirteen years as, she wrote while at the Iowa Writers' Workshop, "a pidgeon-toed [*sic*], only-child with a receding chin and a you-leave-me-alone-or-I'll-bite-you complex." You can climb down a perilously steep set of steps to the backyard to see where she kept her chickens, trace the spot where O'Connor appeared on camera in 1932, fighting to make her "frizzly chicken" behave for the stranger's camera. Upstairs on display is the old claw-foot bathtub, unconnected to any plumbing, where O'Connor would entertain her playmates. O'Connor's frilly baby carriage, a gift from well-to-do relatives, is tucked into the living room, along with the "Kiddie Koop" baby crib where O'Connor slept—a mesh container that looks like an oversized hamster enclosure. You can see a small collection of O'Connor's early literary criticism scrawled on the flaps of her childhood books. (On *Alice's Adventures in Wonderland*: "Awful. I wouldn't read this book." On *Little Men*: "First rate, splendid.")

But aside from these early examples of O'Connor's candor, the house in Savannah has little indication of the stuff that would consume her fiction, the obsessions and religious conviction and dark, moving portraits of the rural, Depression-era South. O'Connor did not return to Savannah often after her parents relocated to Milledgeville, a sleepy mid-sized town in the center of the state where Regina O'Connor had family, the kind of relatives who were heavy hitters in the societal and political workings of the town. Milledgeville had served as the Georgia capital during the Civil War, and the first house O'Connor and her mother lived in there was the Cline Mansion, the former governor's mansion.

It was also the site of a state hospital formerly known as the Milledgeville Lunatic Asylum. In local parlance, "going to Milledgeville" translated to "going crazy." It was also the site of the Georgia State College for Women, now Georgia College & State University, where O'Connor later studied social sciences and drew cartoons for the student newspaper. But perhaps the most welcoming characteristic of Milledgeville for O'Connor was its designation, in 1934, as a bird sanctuary. The city fathers elected to formalize this distinguishing mark in the matter-of-fact town motto, erecting signs downtown that boasted, "Milledgeville: A Bird Sanctuary."

In later letters to her friends, O'Connor would sometimes add the distinction as a flourish on her return address, or as part of an invitation. It became an epithet. She sometimes ran the words together to formulate the e. e. cummings–esque term "birdsanctuary." It was an affectionate rib at her town, a place that often amused O'Connor with its citizens' high estimation of their home. After all, very few parts of Georgia were exactly hostile to birds. To one friend, O'Connor wrote, "We expect you to visit again in Milledgeville, a Bird Sanctuary, where all is culture, graciousness, refinement and bidnis-like common sense." (To another, she wrote, "Greetings from historic Milledgeville where the ladies and gents wash in separate tubs.") But there was also something sincere in O'Connor's embrace of the term, the religious tinge of the word "sanctuary." Because

Milledgeville became, for O'Connor, exactly that: a safe haven, a sacred place, a shelter, and a shrine.

It's fair to say that O'Connor's eventual confinement to Milledgeville was not part of her original plans. "I was roped and tied and resigned the way it is necessary to be resigned to death," she explained in a letter to her friend Maryat Lee. "I thought it would be the end of any creation, any writing." When she was forced to return to her mother's care in Georgia at age twenty-five, O'Connor had been on track to have a flourishing academic and literary career up North. She had graduated from the Iowa Writers' Workshop, where she first arrived with a fifteen-pound muskrat fur coat slung over her arm, with connections to the likes of Southern literature champion and author Andrew Lytle and Robert Penn Warren. It was at Iowa that O'Connor asked her mother's permission to go by "Flannery" instead of "Mary Flannery," in anticipation of having her work published because, she joked to an interviewer, "Who was likely to buy the stories of an Irish washerwoman?" She spent two months at the famed Saratoga Springs artist retreat, Yaddo, where she worked on her first novel, *Wise Blood*. When the first symptoms of systemic lupus erythematosus, the hereditary autoimmune disorder that would ultimately end her life, began to manifest, O'Connor was living in Redding, Connecticut, with friends Robert and Sally Fitzgerald. "I stayed away from the time I was 20 until I was 25 with the notion that the life of my writing depended on my staying away," O'Connor wrote. "I would certainly have persisted in that delusion had I not got very ill and had to come home. The best of my writing has been done here."

The restraints of O'Connor's illness, which she initially believed to be arthritis, also led to Flannery and Regina O'Connor's relocation from the Cline Mansion to the place that would become home for the final thirteen years of O'Connor's life. The move was supposed to be a temporary, practical measure. With O'Connor too weak to handle the staircases at the Cline Mansion, she and her mother took up residence in the 550-acre farm four miles outside of downtown Milledgeville that O'Connor's uncle Bernard Cline had left to Regina and her brother. They set up in the bottom floor of the two-story house on the estate to allow O'Connor to convalesce without bothering with the stairs. When O'Connor and her cousins had visited the place during her summers growing up, it had been called Sorrel Farm, after the reddish coats of the horses her uncle kept there. But on a bus ride to Atlanta, O'Connor met a descendant of the farm's original owner, who told her an earlier name for the farm, which stuck: Andalusia.

THE ONLY BIRDS visible on my approach to Milledgeville were clutches of vultures picking at roadkill on the sides of the highway. The usual roadside exit attractions of the state were in full effect: pecan palaces, peach stands hawking homemade chow-chow (a kind of Southern relish made from green tomatoes) and moonshine jelly (preserves made with white wine, sugar, and gelatin, meant for spreading on toast), pokey billboards offering religious guidance, satellite dishes that dwarfed the neighboring houses. Endless clots of pine trees sprang from the reddened clay. On my stop for late lunch, in a pub in Dublin, Georgia, the bartender professed not to know much about O'Connor. But, he said, he had run into a more recent celebrity resident of the Milledgeville area at an annual event called the Redneck Games: reality star Honey Boo Boo Thompson, a hyperactive child beauty-pageant contestant best known for her preferred meals of ketchup-drenched spaghetti and Red Bull mixed with Mountain Dew. She is, in fact, a character who might feel at home in an O'Connor short story.

To O'Connor, Andalusia Farm had seemed far from the neatly arranged checkerboard of downtown Milledgeville, in the rural hinterlands. The novelist Alice Walker grew up in Eatonton, not far from O'Connor's farm, the daughter of sharecroppers who struggled to support Walker's education and escape from the oppressive rule of Jim Crow. Walker's brother, Jimmy, remembered delivering milk to O'Connor. These days, Andalusia Farm is in the thick of the suburbs and subdivisions surrounding the city. The turn for the farm is closest to several car dealerships, a Comfort Suites, and a Walmart, with a familiar tangle of vinyl siding

and gas stations, fast food joints, and pawnshops surrounding the site. The sign pointing up a sloped drive
to Andalusia was so unassuming that I drove past it
twice, unable to quite fathom plunging into the bank of
pines where the farmhouse stood. As the car crept up
the drive to the white house, the noise of the highway
evaporated, blocked by the dense forest surrounding
the grounds, the trunks of trees wound with kudzu. In
its place grew a lush, leafy silence, punctuated by the
twittering of birds overhead and the occasional mysterious cawing floating in through the car's open window.

During O'Connor's time at Andalusia, the property's
hundreds of acres were bustling with activity. Regina
O'Connor plunged into managing the place first as a
dairy farm and then as a beef-cattle business. She spent
her time split between caring for her daughter and
tending to the many needs of the dozens of cows and
the farmhands who worked with them: mending fences,
keeping books, gauging the health of the cattle. Flannery O'Connor, weakened by multiple blood transfu-
sions and stiffness in her arms and legs from her lupus,
was mostly an observer of the business of the farm. The
house, at the top of the hill, afforded O'Connor a view
of the goings-on from the porch, a vantage point where
she could drink in the exchanges between the people
who labored with the cattle. "I watch what goes on . . .
largely through the crack in the door," O'Connor wrote
in a letter. "My contribution amounts to picking up a

few eggs . . . anyway there is always something going on on a farm to watch."

She busied herself with writing and rewriting from her room downstairs, content to exclude herself from the nitty-gritty of farming. In her story "The Enduring Chill," a semiautobiographical account of a young man named Asbury, fallen ill and forced to take up residence at his mother's farm, O'Connor describes him surveying a farm almost identical to Andalusia from a rocking chair on the screen porch:

> The lawn extended for a quarter of an acre down to a barbed-wire fence that divided it from the front pasture. In the middle of the day the dry cows rested there under a line of sweetgum trees. On the other side of the road were two hills with a pond between and his mother could sit on the porch and watch the herd walk across the dam to the hill on the other side. The whole scene was rimmed by a wall of trees which, at the time of the day he was forced to sit there, was a washed-out blue that reminded him sadly of the Negroes' faded overalls.

The view is now crowded over with thicket, the pasture unsullied by cows. The bustle of farm activity is long gone from Andalusia. But the wall of trees O'Connor described obscures the Walmart and gas stations beyond, making Andalusia feel as it must have to the young writer: an island, where the waves of modernity lap gently at the boundaries but never quite touch.

AFTER HALF A MILE or so of the forest tunnel that leads up from the highway, the drive opens up into the central farm complex, where the plantation house that O'Connor lived in stands proudly, topped by a red metal roof sunbaked by the relentless Georgia rays. A white water tower looms behind. Magnolia trees are lined obediently near the drive, their blooms already faded to the color of old newspapers. The grounds of Andalusia are now a nature preserve, much as those surrounding Faulkner's house at Rowan Oak. There are trails for hiking. Bird watching, naturally, is encouraged. A pamphlet at the house lists the kinds of birds that you might encounter at Andalusia, from wild turkey to the blue-gray gnatcatcher to the loggerhead shrike. Classes from Georgia College & State University occasionally visit the grounds to study local wildlife or the Tobler Creek, which intersects the grounds and was used in the eighteenth century as an avenue for bootleggers.

Though the house has survived more or less intact, not all of the structures on the grounds are as well preserved. The satellite buildings behind the house lie in various states of disarray. The milk-processing shed, the old pump house, and a tenant-farmer residence have been restored, but several other small structures have been reduced to little more than piles of splintered timber. The cow barn, in the midst of restoration, teeters uncertainly, planks of wood missing from its face. There was something slightly menacing and fantastical about it, the hayloft yawning widely at the top of the structure, a rickety, narrow ladder reaching into the darkness. A sign reading DANGER PLEASE DO NOT ENTER was propped up in a dusty white chair near the entrance. O'Connor's crooked Bible salesman from "Good Country People" could have come sprinting out at any minute, carrying a pilfered wooden leg.

Unlike Welty's or Faulkner's houses, O'Connor's last residence was not converted into an official museum until almost forty years after her death. It had remained, for many years, a working farm and an object of curiosity. There are several accounts, including one by Alice Walker, of O'Connor admirers skipping past the No Trespassing signs to marvel at the grounds, but Andalusia only opened to visitors in 2003, after O'Connor's cousins Margaret Florencourt Mann and Louise Florencourt established the Andalusia Foundation in her honor. There was a pleasingly ragged feeling to the endeavor. Rather than being meticulously monitored and scrubbed, things had been allowed to decay and warp with age. It was not hard to imagine O'Connor and her mother still living there, like some middle-Georgia version of *Grey Gardens*, as things quietly fell into disrepair around them. My reveries on the matter were interrupted, suddenly, by a flat, insistent, almost nasal squawk. I walked to the other side of the house, hidden from view from my vantage in the driveway, to find a sizable coop rustling with activities. I had found the peacocks.

THE CHICKENS IN Savannah were just O'Connor's beginner birds. On Andalusia there were already chickens, ducks, geese, and quail; O'Connor tended to them all. But the arrival of the peacocks followed two events that shaped the last decade of O'Connor's life. The first was the publication of her first novel, *Wise Blood*, originally titled *The Great Spotted Bird*. The book was the one that she started while at the Iowa Writers' Workshop, and had worked on in the years living in Yaddo, in Connecticut, and upon her return to Milledgeville. In it, O'Connor announced clearly the themes that she would examine throughout her work: sin and salvation, tolerance and zealotry, the connection between spiritual and physical ailments.

In her satirical tale, the veteran Hazel Motes, fresh off a four-year stint in the Army, grapples with religion in the fictional town of Taulkinham. "He saw Jesus move from tree to tree in the back of his mind," O'Connor wrote, "a wild ragged figure motioning him to turn around and come off into the dark where he was not sure of his footing, where he might be walking on water and not know it and then suddenly know it and drown." Motes turns into a street preacher for the gospel of atheism, encounters a nymphomaniac, a con man, and a mummified dwarf, and eventually blinds himself with quicklime to live as an ascetic. Critical reception of the novel was tepid. Reviewers dismissed O'Connor as one in a line of regional writers penning paeans to oddballs, or else they found the tale impenetrable. But the assessments in newspapers were not as contentious as the reception from O'Connor's relatives. One of her Savannah cousins, the matriarch Katie Semmes, had ordered advance copies for a handful of Catholic priests with whom she was friendly. After *Wise Blood* came out, rumor has it that Semmes shut herself in for a week writing notes of apologies to the clergymen. In person, O'Connor maintained the codes of Southern manners that Milledgeville society required. But her fiction, *Wise Blood* clearly communicated, would not be polite.

The second event was O'Connor's friend Sally Fitzgerald revealing the true diagnosis of her condition. It was not, as she had been told, rheumatoid arthritis, but systemic lupus erythematosus, the same disease that had killed O'Connor's father when she was just fifteen. O'Connor had witnessed her father's deterioration as a young teenager. She knew that the ravages of the autoimmune disease meant that she likely did not have many years left to live. It also meant that O'Connor's stay at Andalusia would be not a temporary measure but a permanent one. O'Connor was forced into several weeks' bed rest after a flare-up of the disease. It was a devastating blow, but one that O'Connor accepted with grace. "I have enough energy to write with and as that is all I have any business doing anyhow, I can with one eye squinted take it all as a blessing," she wrote Fitzgerald.

During the time she was laid up, O'Connor perused an advertisement in the Florida *Market Bulletin* for peafowl at $65 a pair, one that had long intrigued her. She finally seized on the opportunity in October 1952, ordering a peacock and a peahen with four small "peabiddies," to be delivered via railway express.

Once they arrived in Andalusia, the peafowl population quickly proliferated, much to the distress of O'Connor's mother. In "The King of the Birds," written almost a decade after she acquired her first peafowl, O'Connor assessed the situation thus:

It is hard to tell the truth about this bird. The habits of any peachicken left to himself would hardly be noticeable, but multiplied by forty, they become a situation. I was correct that my peachickens would all eat Startena; they also eat everything else. Particularly they eat flowers. My mother's fears were all borne out. Peacocks not only eat flowers, they eat them systematically, beginning at the head of a row and going down it. If they are not hungry, they will pick the flower anyway, if it is attractive, and let it drop. . . . In short, I am the only person on the place who is willing to underwrite, with something more than tolerance, the presence of peafowl.

At their peak, nearly fifty peafowl strutted around the grounds of Andalusia, their long elegant tails trailing through the Georgia dirt. The birds roosted in the trees near the house and brought down the fencing around the cattle pens with their weight. The clatter and clamor of peacocks crying and the sight of their shimmering tail feathers drooped over trash-can lids, fences, and shrubberies, became one of the hallmarks of Andalusia. Once O'Connor made a name for herself, authors would travel to meet her at Andalusia, picking through the peacocks and their droppings to pay a call to the author. "Visitors to our place," O'Connor wrote, "instead of being barked at by dogs rushing from under the porch, are squalled at by peacocks whose blue necks and crested heads pop up from behind tufts of grass, peer out of bushes and crane downward from the roof of the house, where the bird has flown, perhaps for the view." Katherine Anne Porter, who stopped by after reading in nearby Macon, "plowed all over the yard behind me in spike-heeled shoes to see my various kind of chickens," O'Connor wrote.

O'Connor collected the feathers from the birds when they molted in the late summer and sent them in care packages to her friends, sometimes alongside freshly collected pecans. She donated some of the plumes to the ladies of Milledgeville, who wore them in their hats, and doled out the pinions to children visiting the farm. On her gravestone, in the Memory Hill Cemetery, fans sometimes leave peacock feathers in tribute.

The most famous photographs of O'Connor, taken by photojournalist Joe McTyre for the *Atlanta Constitution*, show her leaning on the crutches that doctors recommended starting in 1955, a pair of peacocks turned in attention. Her daily routine involved working daily from nine a.m. to noon, the space that her illness would allow, and spending the afternoon painting, rocking on the front porch, observing her ostentation of peacocks. The feathers became her personal symbol, shorthand for her work.

Peacocks, as O'Connor well knew, have transformative powers. For O'Connor, the peacock's display was not just a natural wonder but also a reminder of the existence of a higher power. "You can't have a peacock anywhere without having a map of the universe," O'Connor explained in a letter. "It also stands in the medieval symbology of the Church—the eyes are the eyes of the Church." For the devoutly Catholic O'Connor, the peacock was a symbol for the wonders that lie just beyond the realm of vision, the possibility of the divine. They were a link between the physical and the ethereal worlds, the same connection that she explored in her fiction, of the freakish qualities of humanity as a spiritual journey made manifest. And they were a promise, too, that creatures of all kinds are more than what they appear to be.

Captured in these birds is also something of the public perception of O'Connor as an outsider. She seemed an exotic creature living in a humble environment, someone whose stark, sharp, odd voice punctured the pleasant myths that Southern writers swathed themselves in. In one of the self-portraits O'Connor painted, of herself in a straw hat posed next to a pheasant, her representation is strikingly birdlike: the shirt the same rust color as the bird's breast, their eyes both set ahead. The birds of Hera squawking alongside the tree frogs in middle Georgia captured something essential about the contrasts in O'Connor's persona: a Southern woman fluent in the graces of society, whose fiction portrayed a singular, searing vision.

THE PEACOCKS IN Andalusia today are more contained than the ones that ran around the premises in O'Connor's final years. When I approached the truck-sized pen, the peahens, scratching at the ground, looked up in alarm. The humidity felt like being swathed in thick, damp cotton, and the whine of mosquitoes Dopplered in and out of earshot. The peacock, its feathers gold and green under a coating of dust, fluttered up to perch on a small bench and emitted a trilling caw, the one that O'Connor had compared to "a cheer for an invisible parade." The birds, all three of them contained in a spacious aviary, looked suspiciously at me before returning to the business of pecking at the dirt. A black-and-white sign posted to the cage instructed visitors: PLEASE DON'T FEED OR FRIGHTEN THE BIRDS.

I turned from the enclosure and trudged back

toward the house, anticipating the sweet, metallic chill of air conditioning. I trudged up the steep steps and through the door of the screen porch, and was greeted by a man with blond hair and a wide grin. "I see y'all have been getting acquainted," he said, nodding to the peacocks.

He introduced himself as Craig Amason, a former librarian who had been appointed the first executive director of the Flannery O'Connor–Andalusia Foundation. He has been at the house since before it was opened, though he was in his final months in the position there. (Elizabeth Wylie succeeded Amason later that year; she has plans to restore the Andalusia backyard in a similar fashion to Welty's garden, by using the descriptions from O'Connor in her essays and letters.) Amason and visitor-services manager Mark Jurgensen were in charge of the operations at the farm, Amason tells me, including minding the peacocks. The birds dined on game feed, cracked corn, grapes, and baby spinach. Jurgensen documented their antics on the Andalusia blog, referring fondly to the "scraggly squawkers" and tracking their molting season, spent "raking up feathers by the wheelbarrowful."

The birds are not descendants of O'Connor's pride. Those, Regina O'Connor dispersed after Flannery's death: One pair to a hospice, one to Stone Mountain Park outside of Atlanta, another to a monastery. A peacock's life-span is only about twenty years, so any of O'Connor's original companions would have likely died off in the 1980s. The last of the farm animals that had descended from Regina's stock, a hinny named Flossie, had died in 2010. Andalusia's current muster of peacocks arrived in 2009, thanks to a donor. Their names were culled from O'Connor's works. I had just met Manley Pointer, Joy/Hulga, and Mary Grace.

The tour of the Andalusia house was a self-guided affair, though Amason encouraged questions. The viewing area was limited to the bottom floor, the portion of the house that O'Connor mostly occupied. The rooms are modestly furnished, faded rugs covering the floors. The paint was peeling in parts of the rooms. Amason pointed out the drapes in one room, hemmed with particularly long stitches, explaining that Regina O'Connor had likely made the alteration in haste in order to return to her many other duties on the farm. The Hotpoint refrigerator in the back kitchen was the one that O'Connor had bought her mother with the television rights for "The Life You Save May Be Your Own."

O'Connor's room was a small, almost monastic affair. It housed a single bed with a thin patterned coverlet. "We want it to be like she just left out the back door," Amason said. "The only major things missing are her books and papers." O'Connor's crutches were leaned against the wardrobe. Her desk, simple and wooden, was pushed up against a window. A replica of O'Connor's typewriter—a squat gray-green number—perched at attention on the desk's surface. On the original—now housed along with her christening gown, walnut bookshelves, and a couple of other personal effects at the Georgia State College for Women—O'Connor would devotedly type out her daily allotment of words. She described her setup to a friend thus: "I have a large ugly brown desk, one of those that the typewriter sits in a depression in the middle of and on either side are drawers." Missing from the scene were the "rat's nest of old papers, clippings, torn manuscripts, ancient quarterlies" that O'Connor built around herself. But the most crucial aspect of the arrangement was the proximity to the window, allowing O'Connor to eavesdrop on the farm workers.

After the publication of *Wise Blood*, O'Connor's fiction began to take on a different tone. Life at Andalusia quickly became fuel for a series of short stories, some inspired by chatter overheard from the tenant families and various visitors. The window in front of O'Connor's desk looked out on the farm complex, allowing her to casually spy on their comings and goings. In one letter to Sally Fitzgerald, O'Connor described a dairyman who, she wrote, "calls all the cows *he*: he ain't give but two gallons, he ain't come in yet. . . . I reckon he doesn't like to feel surrounded by females or something." The habits and mannerisms of middle-Georgia folk were rhythms that O'Connor adapted into her own writing. Like Eudora Welty, O'Connor kept note of local parlance that tickled her, particularly names. A Lucynell who attended O'Connor's book signing for *Wise Blood* appeared in "The Life You Save May Be Your Own" as

Lucynell Crater, a deaf-mute with "eyes as blue as a peacock's neck." The fugitive bank robber in "A Good Man Is Hard to Find" got his name, "The Misfit," from a clipping O'Connor found in the *Journal-Constitution* with a similar alias. One visitor, Father James McCown, later recalled that when he was asking directions to Andalusia, a Milledgeville lady reported, "Mary Flannery is a sweet girl. But I'm afraid to go near her. She might put me in one of her stories."

It was in the short stories that O'Connor wrote at Andalusia where her gift for intercepting and shaping language flourished. The smaller scope concentrated her style, increased her potency. It was in them that she created her most indelible characters—the family in "A Good Man Is Hard to Find," with a mother "whose face was as broad and innocent as a cabbage," and the overeducated innocent Joy/Hulga in "Good Country People." She caught the middle-Georgia dialect exactly: point A to point B nonstop is going "terreckly," and the British royal family included the "Duchesser Windsor." Even the titles of her stories had a pleasing lilt to them, the kinds of religious-tinged wisdom dropped as conversation starters and stoppers between people: "You Can't Be Any Poorer Than Dead" and "The Life You Save May Be Your Own." In a recording of O'Connor reading "A Good Man Is Hard to Find" at Vanderbilt University in 1959, she pauses to savor certain words and is forced to stop for a moment thanks to waves of laughter at the joking passages. Once I heard the recording, every story

I read by O'Connor included her Georgia drawl, the distinct voice that she had faithfully re-created.

If most people know O'Connor through her stories and not her essays and longer work, it is partially because the stories are, by nature of their form, more easily digestible than novels or discourses about the Catholic writer. But partly it is because many of them are extraordinarily effective at fulfilling the O'Connor doctrine that acolytes like Harry Crews would later take to heart: that the best way of capturing people's attention was through unsettling and enduring characters. She did not hope to placate or comfort, but to gut her readers by laying out the assumptions and faulty logical systems and petty cruelties that humanity operates on. And O'Connor resented the implication that this tactic was a cheap one. She complained in one lecture that the label of "Southern Gothic" had reduced her and other writers to "unhappy combinations of Poe and Erskine Caldwell."

Her distortion was a kind of realism: She sought to make the moral blemishes and weaknesses every person carries visible to the naked eye. "We have become so flooded with sorry fiction based on unearned liberties . . . that in the public mind the deeper kinds of realism are less and less understandable," O'Connor noted in a speech later published as "The Grotesque in Southern Fiction." The kind of writing she aimed for was closer to the aims of cubists, attempting to see every facet of an individual on one plane. "It is not necessary to point out that the look of this fiction is going to be wild, that it is almost of necessity going to be violent and comic, because of the discrepancies that it seeks to combine," she continued.

O'Connor, like Harper Lee and Eudora Welty, was often portrayed as a hermit in the press, thanks to the remoteness of Milledgeville from New York City or Los Angeles. But O'Connor, when illness would allow her, traveled to give lectures and readings as her work began to gain popularity. Though Andalusia was on the outskirts, Regina and Flannery O'Connor frequented the social set of Milledgeville. She and her mother went to Mass at the Sacred Heart Catholic Church. O'Connor met on Wednesdays with a book group, and dined regularly at the Sanford House, a high dining establishment with a copy of the Ordinance of Secession, the Civil War–era document formally announcing that Georgia had seceded from the Union, printed on a silk banner and hung in the entrance hall. O'Connor's favorite menu selection was the peppermint chiffon pie. Though O'Connor's writing caused a minor scandal among the ladies who lunch, she was accepted into the inner circle as a member of her mother's family, the Clines. It's this acceptance that gave an extra acidity to O'Connor's writing, an insider perspective on the enforcement of manners and the idea of Southern nobility. O'Connor's fiction is a reproach to the idea that manners are protection, a shredding of the self-perpetuating mythos of the South. O'Connor was not interested in the image of the South as a simpler, more virtuous place.

"I am always vastly irritated by these people . . . who know as much about the South as I do about lower Hobokin [*sic*] and on the strength of it advise Southern writers to leave it and forget the myth," she wrote in a letter. "Which myth? If you're a writer and the South is what you know, then it's what you'll write about and how you judge it will depend on how you judge yourself. . . . So much depends on what you have an ear for. . . . The advantages and disadvantages of being a Southern writer can be endlessly debated but the fact remains that if you are, you are."

O'Connor's Catholic beliefs provided her work with a blistering equality: Northerners, Southerners, men, and women are all equally corrupt, equally struggling toward grace. She was haunted not by the racial past of the region but by the unrelenting judgment of an omnipotent God. The women have fat ankles and nasal voices, not delicate feet and sweeping petticoats. The men are ugly and petty. She does not do her characters the flattery and disservice of gussying them up; they are all caught equally. In her essay about her visit to O'Connor's house, Alice Walker wrote that she considered O'Connor the first great Southern modernist, "Because when she set her pen to [her characters] not a whiff of magnolia hovered in the air." Walker continued, "Yes, I could say, these white folks without the magnolia . . .

and these black folks without melons and superior racial patience, these are like the Southerners I know."

MILLEDGEVILLE SOCIETY'S MIXED reception of O'Connor's work—acknowledging her as one of their own but wishing she could have written something more ladylike—remains today. O'Connor's cousins, the Florencourts and their descendants, remain fixtures of Milledgeville, and are involved in preserving her legacy. But there is the sense, while asking around in town, that O'Connor's work is strange and alienating. "That's some pretty weird stuff," one store clerk told me when I asked about her.

There are, of course, many who celebrate O'Connor's work, who travel to Milledgeville to study her archives. Since her death in August 1963, O'Connor's literary star has risen. The house averages some 5,000 visitors a year, many of whom react emotionally to the experience. Amason recalled one woman weeping as she stared into the little bedroom where O'Connor slept and worked. One couple even elected to get married at the farm. The bride wore peacock feathers woven through her hair.

I crept toward the back of the house to the gift shop, located near the tiny kitchen. Alongside the usual selection of books and postcards, there was an array of peacock-related items: ornaments, journals, earrings. Another section held pieces of reliquary available to commemorate the visit. A vase held plumes from Manley Pointer's tail, collected last molting season and available for $5 each. Vials of dirt from the farm were also for sale, along with rosary beads and bumper stickers. One read A GOOD MAN IS HARD TO FIND—MILLEDGEVILLE, GA. Another, SEE 'FOWL PLAY' AT ANDALUSIA FARM IN MILLEDGEVILLE, GA.

In "The Fiction Writer & His Country," O'Connor tackles the idea of Southern writers as provincial creatures, bound up in their obsessive cataloguing of local color.

> When we talk about the writer's country we are liable to forget that no matter what particular country it is, it is inside as well as outside of him. Art requires a delicate adjustment of the inner and outer worlds in such a way that, without changing their nature, they can be seen through each other. To know oneself is to know one's region. It is also to know the world, and it is also, paradoxically, a form of exile from that world.

Andalusia became the place of O'Connor's exile in Milledgeville, but it also became her place of greatest imaginative strength. She turned a little dairy farm in Georgia into a preserve for herself and her birds, odd creatures in an odd land. She absorbed the country around her, and inscribed her own vision of the world upon it.

I headed by the aviary to bid farewell to the flock. The peahens emitted a cacophony of coos and cries that echoed out into the nearby woods, their feet scratching out patterns into the dust. "It is a great blessing, perhaps the greatest blessing a writer can have, to find at home what others have to go elsewhere seeking," O'Connor writes. It was this small patch of land, in the peripheral vision of these birds, that O'Connor had found what she was seeking, spinning the place into her prose. The peacock, Manley, strutted over to the side of the pen to inspect my hand for food. Finding nothing, he squawked once in indignation and then paused, as if considering his next move. His tail feathers glimmered in the dying light, reminders of the glory he could unfurl with a fanning out of his coat. And then he turned, clucking, away, his claws scratching strange hieroglyphics in the soil of the writer's country.

5.   Harry Crews's Hurricane Creek
BACON COUNTY, GA

Three hours south of Milledgeville, in the part of Georgia just seventy miles shy of the Florida line, is Bacon County, a rural patch of the state where novelist Harry Crews grew up. Crews was an acolyte of O'Connor; he considered her one of his greatest heroes. His fiction is full of the freaks that O'Connor loved, great-grandchildren of Hazel Motes and Manley Pointer. Crews was particularly fond of the dictum O'Connor set forth in "The Fiction Writer & His Country," one he often quoted: "When you can assume that your audience holds the same beliefs as you do, you can relax a little and use more normal means of talking to it; when you have to assume that it does not, then you have to make your vision apparent by shock—to the hard of hearing you shout, and to the near-blind, you draw large and startling figures."

THERE IS NO MEMORIAL to Harry Crews in Bacon County, Georgia. No markers point out the patch of land where the tiny county's most famous resident grew up; no street has been renamed in his honor; no bronze statue of Crews's battle-worn figure adorns the bench of a local park. A mural in Alma, the largest city in Bacon

County, includes portraits of dancing blueberries and a depiction of a red Viking raider, the high school's mascot, but no trace of Crews. Where other Southern towns clutch at chances to promote themselves as tourist destinations for booklovers, Bacon County shrugs. Even the library in Alma, the natural place for the celebration of local writers, has little trace of Crews. A single shelf in the back holds an incomplete collection of Crews's works; a manila folder in the cupboard-sized archives rooms preserves a few halfhearted reviews of his books and a smattering of announcements about Crews cutting a ribbon for a local ceremony or passing through to research. For a devotee of Crews's fiction, it is odd to be met with such indifference at the source of his writing. After all, Crews's entire life's work is a monument to Bacon County.

If the residents of Bacon County, on the whole, don't harbor as much affection for Crews as the population of Oxford does for Faulkner, it's likely due to a combination of Crews's cantankerousness, the graphically unpleasant nature of much of his fiction, and his unflinching, often unflattering description of the place where he grew up. In his dazzling memoir *A Childhood: The Biography of a Place,* Crews introduces himself as "a boy who was raised in the rickets-and-hookworm belt of South Georgia." He begins his life's story with an account of how his father contracted gonorrhea from a Seminole prostitute.

Crews's fiction is full of the nastier underbelly of this

rural life: dogfights and drunks, snake handlers and wife beaters, the cruelty of the land and the perversity of its inhabitants hopelessly intertwined with their generosity and beauty. Without fail his characters end up shredded, sometimes emotionally but most often physically: the failed high school football player Joe Lon in *A Feast of Snakes* torn apart by a writhing mess of serpents after opening fire on a rattlesnake festival; the faith healer of *The Gospel Singer* lynched by his former followers; the automobile obsessive in *Car* who destroys his digestive tract by attempting eat a whole Cadillac. *All We Need of Hell* begins with a man, mid-coitus, picturing stealing a potato from a fellow captive in Auschwitz. In *A Feast of Snakes,* a black woman driven into psychosis lops off the penis of the one-legged sheriff who raped her, believing it to be a rattlesnake. The worlds Crews constructs are hellish, populated by people with deep scars and quick tempers.

Shock is a tool that Crews mastered and employed with precision. There is joy in his shouting, a tabloidesque love for the sensational and the bizarre, and a need to shake his reader out of the lull of their perceptions, to jostle them loose of the air-conditioned confines of middle-class suburbia. His aim is to force his readers to confront their squeamishness, like a boy on the playground handing a pile of grubby worms to a little girl in a frilly dress. For Crews, this was a necessary function of fiction. It is through the challenges of violence and atrocity that the tenderness of human nature is exposed.

Like O'Connor, Crews is preoccupied by physical deformity; his books are crowded with deaf-mutes, midgets, men with consuming skin diseases, the hideously obese. When interviewers questioned him about the freaks in his books, Crews would often give a nod to the photographer Diane Arbus, whom he admired for taking pictures of her unbeautiful subjects straight-on. Crews's fondness for these characters, some of them inspired by time he spent working with a carnival freak show, stems from the belief that outer disfigurements are only expressions of the conflicts all people suffer made flesh. "I have never been able to forgive myself the grotesqueries and aberrations I am able to hide with such impunity in my own life," Crews wrote, echoing Arbus's conviction that freaks are simply born with the trauma everyone ultimately faces. At heart, we are all freaks. "I am convinced that you and I, all of us, are caught in the same kind of inexplicable, almost blind terror," Crews told a French reporter. "Except that ours is not so apparent."

Crews's writing is unrelenting, intentionally disturbing, caustic, pitiless, and often awful in its honesty. At its best, it is also beautiful, and wickedly funny. It is an open rebuke to the romance of the rural South, a splattering of turpentine on the meticulously painted gloss of the place. But it is still not the kind of fiction discussed at most family dinner tables. Even Crews's older brother Hoyett refused to read any of Crews's writing, declaring it "pornographic." When I mentioned Crews's writing to a waitress at a restaurant I had stopped into for lunch in Alma, she raised her eyebrows in mock alarm. "You read those books? Oo—ee!" she exclaimed. Little wonder that the politicians of Alma aren't keen to rename their town square after him.

HARRY CREWS DIED IN 2012, after spending most of his life a little less than three hours south of Alma, teaching creative writing at the University of Florida and churning out fiction with an awe-inspiring combination of fervor and discipline. He first came to Gainesville after a three-year stint in the Marine Corps allowed him to enroll in the University of Florida in 1956 on the GI Bill, and settled there after a meandering motorcycle trip across the country and a year teaching junior high English in Jacksonville. There the renowned Tennessee writer and teacher Andrew Lytle took him under his wing and shaped Crews as a writer and a teacher. It's Gainesville where Crews became town legend, where he picked fights in pool halls and woke up with new scars, where he pounded out a voluminous number of books, articles, and syllabi. It's Gainesville where Crews had two sons with his college sweetheart, Sally, whom he married twice and divorced twice, and where he found his four-year-old firstborn, Patrick, drowned in his neighbor's pool.

In Gainesville, Crews garnered fame as a roughneck poet and deep-fried weirdo, the commander of a new wave of gritty Southern writing that depicted the harshness of rural Georgia without the cushion of metaphor. There, Crews worked to transform the swamps and red clay tracts of his childhood into fictional worlds peppered with humor and horror. You can still find bartenders in town who will gladly tell you tales of Crews's drunken exploits. His former devoted students, who dubbed themselves "Crews's Crew," will recount his pearls of wisdom and standoffs with school officials. One of Crews's former pupils, Jay Atkinson, wrote in his book *Memoirs of a Rugby-Playing Man* an account about his first day under the writer's instruction, in which Crews casually challenged him to a fistfight after Atkinson slighted his speaking style. The matter was settled after Atkinson submitted a piece of fiction that his professor approved of.

Crews was never a household name, but he gained some measure of fame as a literary wild man, a cult writer with moxie. Most of this reputation stemmed from the nonfiction he wrote, rambling first-person accounts of dogfights and bar brawls. He wrote a column for *Esquire* and competed for *Playboy* assignments with Norman Mailer, once traveling to Valdez, Alaska, to write about the construction of an oil pipeline, only to wake up hungover in a rental car with a cabinet hinge tattooed in the crook of his right elbow. (He expensed the ink. "Hugh Hefner paid $60 for that tattoo," Crews liked to joke.) Crews befriended Sean Penn, and went on to make a cameo as a bereaved father named Mr. Baker in Penn's directorial debut *The Indian Runner* before dedicating his novel *Scar Lover* to the star. Elvis Presley was rumored to be considering playing the title role in a screen adaptation of *The Gospel Singer*. Crews took Rip Torn on a Florida alligator hunt, and Sonic Youth's Kim Gordon and Teenage Jesus and the Jerk's Lydia Lunch named a side project after him (the album they released in 1989, *Naked in Garden Hills*, was named after Crews's second novel). But outside of urban literary circles and a certain Hollywood set, Crews's fame remained localized to Florida and Georgia, and he was largely content to keep it that way, laboring on his writing while maintaining a reputation as an author better not messed with.

Still, Crews had the kind of personality that invited trouble, and a macho reputation that often eclipsed his body of writing. Interviewers would often include a reference to a recent night Crews had spent in jail and an inventory of the damage he had suffered from late night vodka-fueled scraps: a row of teeth knocked out, a crisscross pattern of razor-blade wounds across his chest, a broken nose, a broken neck, a cheekbone flattened by a pool cue. Crews often landed in tangles, it seemed, but rarely won them. In pictures, Crews looks grim and intimidating, his head shaved on either side and styled into a Mohawk, a thick mustache claiming his upper lip. (When Crews appeared on Dennis Miller's show, the host described the look, accurately, as a "G.-Gordon-Liddy-meets-Vanilla-Ice type thing.") His torso was muscled and solid-looking, thanks to dabbling in bodybuilding, karate, and boxing. On his arm,

Crews sported a skull tattoo with a scrap of e.e. cummings poetry referenced menacingly underneath: "How
Do You Like Your Blue-Eyed Boy, Mr. Death?" Crews
crafted this persona—or as he termed his hairdo and
tattoo, the "'do and 'too" combination—with the same
confrontational spirit as his fiction. "It's a psychological truth that before you can make a judgment about
somebody else, you have to make a judgment about
yourself," Crews explained to the University of Florida
alumni magazine in 1992. "People who can't get past
my haircut are people who have already decided what
can be done with hair and what cannot be done with
hair. I designed this haircut myself, and I did it with
malice and forethought." The effect obviously pleased
Crews. "Not many people *laugh* when I'm around," he
told another interviewer from *Southern Quarterly*. "I walk
into the bank and all the guards put their hands on
their guns."

ON A SOJOURN to Gainesville, I met Ted Geltner,
Crews's biographer and friend, for a beer at Lillian's
Music Store, one of the dive bars Crews used to frequent
in the college town. It's the kind of place that it's easy
to imagine Crews in: a popcorn machine lurks in the
corner, the bartenders wear suspenders with musical
notation printed on them, and the décor looks like it
was lifted from a church auction. During a lull in our
conversation, Geltner pointed to a corner across the

street from where we were sitting. "That's where Harry got stabbed," he said, with all the gravity of noting his favorite coffee spot. In Geltner's telling, a fan had come up to Crews and asked who he was. Once confirming the writer's identity, he produced a knife and cut Crews, as a kind of souvenir interaction. The wound wasn't that serious, Geltner assured me. Some fans ask for autographs, but Crews's fans demanded blood—perhaps because blood is the currency Crews most valued. These are the kind of Crews stories that Gainesville is rife with, the ones where he is a cross between Hunter S. Thompson, Lord Byron, and Popeye. Crews mythology floats over Gainesville like a thin fog. He is part of the climate.

But if the fable of Crews belongs to Gainesville, it is Bacon County that has his spirit. Crews's most indelible characters come from that region or just nearby, a place that clearly haunted him long after he had moved across the Florida state line. "I come from people who believe the *home place* is as vital and necessary as the beating of your own heart," Crews wrote in *Childhood*. "Bacon County is my home place, and I've had to make do with it."

WHICH IS HOW I found myself driving on a hot July day up to Bacon County, in search of the places Crews wrote about. On the drive from northern Florida to southern Georgia, the verdant swamp transforms to a black-water one, the highway occasionally giving glimpses at its shimmering, brown-green depths. As you close in on Bacon County, the landscape grows thick with straight-backed longleaf pine trees, tracts of forest so evenly spaced and unyielding they give the impression of a vast platoon of arboreal soldiers, frozen mid-drill. The highway gives way to country roads dotted with signs for taxidermists and advertisements for lodgings near the Okefenokee Swamp, locally deemed to be an excellent site for train watching. Crews had hunted in the swamp as a boy, before the expanse of it had been declared a wildlife preserve. Battered electronic shops sported staggering antennas, signs of the bustling CB radio traffic in these parts. Church signs boast of full gospel choirs, and proclaim biblical wisdom to motorists in aphorisms: FORBIDDEN FRUIT CREATES MANY JAMS, and LIFE IS LIKE TENNIS. YOU CANNOT WIN WITHOUT SERVING.

Childhood is the biography of Bacon County, but it is also a paean for parts of the place as it once was. The span that *Childhood* covers is from 1935, when Crews was born, until the early 1940s. In the seventy years since, most of the structures Crews wrote about disappeared, along with a good chunk of the tobacco, peanut, and cotton farming that had sustained the county. Out of respect for the relatives he wrote about, many of them still living when he published the memoir, Crews left many details about his early years vague.

Though *Childhood* leaves few locations easily identifiable to someone unfamiliar with the community, there are hints. Orienting myself by a stretch of Big Hurricane Creek and Crews's memoir, I sketched a rough map of the places Crews wrote about—one that turned out to be mostly wrong. I drove around in circles, getting out to squint at the creek bed and swat mosquitoes, consulting Crews's book like an outdated star map. The only landmark I successfully located was Ten Mile Missionary Baptist Church, where Crews's mother and father were married, next to the creek where his mother was baptized. The small graveyard out back held the tiny body of Crews's eldest brother, dead shortly after being born, and buried in an unmarked grave. The church had clearly gotten a facelift or two since then. It now featured its own barbecue smoker tucked in the back and a plastic replica of Noah's Ark for children to play on. On the porch of a well-kept house across the street, a squirrel in a wrought-iron cage squeaked furiously.

Likely that frantic squirrel would have marked the end of my hunt if it weren't for a traveling preacher and furniture salesman named Tom Davis, who had grown up with Crews. Though Davis couldn't be my tour guide—his schedule kept him away from Alma—he offered me an introduction to Don Haselden, Crews's younger cousin and the son of Alton Haselden, the man who helped raise Crews after his father died.

Haselden invited me to his house after Sunday supper, directing me to a brick home off the highway, "settin' in the pecan trees." An affable retired farmer with a deep South Georgia drawl that transformed "hurricane" to "harrikin," Haselden has the same gray hair and weather-beaten skin as Crews did. He wore purple-tinted glasses and a red plaid shirt with an array of pens and small hand tools tucked into the breast pocket, a pair of sharp-toed cowboy boots peeking out from under the cuffs of his blue jeans. Haselden had his own collection of scars. His time training horses and mules had left him with a litany of injuries, including a row of metal pins down his neck. Haselden walked hesitantly, with a cane, and occasionally winced midsentence thanks to stinging pain in his back. "I've had fourteen surgeries since eleventh grade of school. I turned sixty-nine this year," Haselden told me. "Or what's left of me."

For a fan of Crews's writing, meeting Haselden is like finally making the acquaintance of someone whose exploits have been recounted to you many times. Haselden doesn't appear in *Childhood* except for the final scene in a tobacco field, where an older Crews, fresh from the Marines, stews with four of his cousins under the Georgia sun. According to Haselden, Crews misremembered the moment: It was Don and not his other cousin Jones who was there with him. "But everyone knows it was me," Haselden said, showing a place in *Childhood* where he had crossed out "Jones" and written "Don," reading aloud the corrected passage proudly. I recognized Haselden through mannerisms and phrases Crews had plucked from his family to garnish his characters, a sensation both reassuring and startling.

Haselden was used to interest in his famous cousin, inquiries from local reporters and the occasional documentary filmmaker. Crews's writing was not for him, he explained, but he was proud of his cousin nonetheless. "I just wasn't raised with that language," Haselden said. "But I admire what he did. He served his country. He educated himself. I admire Harry for what he came from—nothing, like the rest of us." Haselden was happy to burnish the memory of his cousin, and his skill at training mules had earned him some media attention of his own, including a story in the *Tallahassee Democrat*, where a columnist celebrated a particularly ornery mule named Mr. Carter—so vicious that he used to break the necks of goats and eat chickens. Haselden had adopted Mr. Carter and taught him to sit, roll over, and wiggle his ears on command. Haselden presented me, chuckling, with a copy of the column, underlined in several passages. "I've always been a cowboy," he said. He still had Mr. Carter, along with a couple of horses, in the barn out back. Later he would stage a demonstration of Mr. Carter's talents, he promised.

In the living room, Haselden pulled out a box of family photos, pointing out Crews's grinning face alongside a group of cousins: Aurex (pronounced "Ey-roo"), Eugenia, Edward, Roger, and Jones. "Harry was like me, a Georgia bulldog," Haselden said. Crews was ten years older than Haselden, but the two were close. Haselden's father, Alton, was Crews's mother Myrtice's older brother. Myrtice married her first husband, Ray, when she was sixteen and he twenty-three. Ray died when Crews was a few months shy of two years old, and Myrtice married Ray's brother, Pascal, whom Crews believed to be his father for most of his childhood. After Pascal's bouts of drunken violence intensified and Myrtice left him, Alton and his wife, Eva, helped Myrtice raise Crews. "He was like Mom and Daddy's other young'un," Haselden said.

In *Childhood*, Crews describes Alton teaching Crews how to slice open the craw of an ailing rooster, how to set a rabbit trap and noodle for catfish with his bare hands. Crews spent almost every summer at his uncle's house until he enlisted, helping tend the hogs and hunting squirrels in the woods with his cousins. "Harry was a good shot with a .22 rifle," Haselden remembered. "He was good enough he could light a match with it. Once I dared him shoot the curly tail off a black sow. Next you know, she's squealin' down the road, no tail."

As Haselden flipped through the photos, he landed upon one of Crews's mother at age fifteen, shortly before she was married. It was a picture Crews described in *Childhood*, a black-and-white photograph of his mother looking "round and pink and pretty." I recognized it, almost remembered this photo I had never seen before, the same way I felt already acquainted with Don Haselden. I realized that I was learning about Crews's family the same way he did, from ragged-edged photographs and legends well worn as luck charms. While researching *Childhood*, Crews relied on scraps of lore about his father, stories he was too young to witness firsthand. "I have lived with the stories of him so long that they are as true as anything that ever happened to me," Crews wrote. "Nothing is allowed to die in a society of storytelling people."

It is a testament to Crews's prose that he brings his family this close, acquaints his reader well enough that a perfect stranger like me might feel faintly that these are figures of my own memories. The thick crust of Crews's persona, the blackness of his humor, sometimes obscures the beating heart of his writing. But I felt it there, gazing at each document Haselden passed me.

Haselden listened, amused, when I told him of my previous attempt to triangulate where Crews had grown up. "Well, you weren't ever going to find it that way," he told me. "We'll take my truck." We clambered into the cab of an imposing white pickup truck. Rain pattered on the windshield in fits and starts, softening the dirt road we headed down into watery putty that sucked at the tires. As Haselden drove, he pointed out the way the landscape had shifted, recounted how his father used to gather up his neighbors in a dinged-up school bus and make the trip into Alma whenever they needed groceries. A wave of cholera had killed the family's hogs in the 1950s; Haselden pointed out the spot where they had to burn the bodies, unable to use the precious, diseased meat. He stopped at a clearing next to a small blue house, slung low amid a clearing. "See that oak tree?" Haselden asked, gesturing toward an imposing specimen in the yard. I nodded. He nodded back: "That was where the boiler was."

The boiler represents the most harrowing of the near-death experiences Crews recounts in his memoir. It was hog-killing day in 1941, and the boiler, an enormous cast-iron vat heated by a wood fire underneath, was heated so the water was just shy of boiling. Crews's family slipped slaughtered pigs into the water to loosen the coarse bristles from their skin, after which they'd be scraped and butchered, each piece allotted to a different dish. Crews, his brother, and his cousins were playing a game of pop the whip, each of the children all holding hands as the leader sprints and turns suddenly, popping the last link of the human chain loose and sending him flying. Crews, the final link in the chain, lost hold of his cousins and went careening straight into the vat of scalding water. Though rescued from the boiler, Crews was badly burned. "I reached over and touched my right hand with my left, and the whole thing came off like a wet glove," Crews recalls in his memoir. "When my overalls were pulled down, my cooked and glowing skin came down."

Alton and Myrtice rushed Crews to the doctor in town. Though the burns covered almost all of his body, Crews would survive with little treatment. The doctor prescribed a long period of bed rest while the outer layers of skin grew back. Alton built a frame around Crews's bed to keep the covers off him during his recovery, and rigged an electric light to burn over his redraw body, so the skin would dry out and scab. "Daddy covered the frame in cheesecloth, to keep the flies off," Haselden said. "I still don't know how Harry survived it."

It wasn't the first time Crews had been confined to a sickbed in his short life. *Childhood* is a map of traumas survived, untimely ends barely escaped. As a toddler, Crews put a lump of raw lye in his mouth, causing his tongue and mouth to bleed profusely. When he was five, Crews suffered through a mysterious illness that temporarily paralyzed his legs, one that he later speculated was polio. Crews was helpless for six weeks, his legs locked in a kneeling position. He recovered gradually, training himself to walk again by ambling around the house as he steadied himself on the surrounding fence. His childhood injuries and illnesses drew people from around the county over to offer solutions, entertain Crews with stories, and behold his ravaged, tiny body. He learned to "accept the good-natured brutality and savagery in the eyes of those who came to wish me well." A faith healer attempted to right Crews's legs through prayer. Later, Crews would mark these times as the genesis for his sympathy for circus freaks, an understanding of how it felt to be gawped at.

These long stretches of rest also allowed Crews time to absorb gossip as his mother and her friends quilted by the fireplace, the life of the county recounted in quiet conversation. Crews would sit in the corner sucking on a "sugar tit"—a scrap of sacking with a lump of sugar or a dab of cloth soaked in syrup inside, distributed to pacify small children—and listening as the voices of the women kept time with the rhythmic click of their needles against thimbles. "It was always the women who scared me," Crews wrote in *Childhood*. Though both men and women told stories, it was the ladies sitting with the quilting frame whose yarns were "unrelieved by humor and filled with apocalyptic vision." Crews metabolized these stories, began crafting his own tales, thickened with details he took from eavesdropping on the quilting circle. Fantasy was survival, escape, a way to make peace with the claustrophobic confines of the sickbed. One of Crews's favorite pastimes was making up stories about figures in the Sears Roebuck catalog, supplying the neatly outfitted models on the pages with haunted pasts and complicated backgrounds, assuming that the clothes disguised wounds and gnarled limbs.

I snapped a picture of the spot where the boiler had stood, and Haselden drove on. We pulled off the road to a patch of land where a large gray trailer squatted on cement bricks. He honked his horn, a long note echoing in the insistent drizzle that was still coming down. We walked to the door slowly, Haselden leaning on his cane. Mosquitoes clouded around, nipping at his bare arms. "I don't know who lives here now, but I'll find out," he said. He knocked on the door, and a little girl peeked out curiously, her mother a step behind her. Haselden introduced himself. "This land is where my cousin was born," he told them, pointing to the trees surrounding the trailer with his cane. "We'll just be a little while." The woman nodded her assent.

The land we were standing on was the old Cash Carter place, two hundred acres Crews's father, Ray, had farmed until he died of a heart attack, worked to exhaustion. The house Crews was born in, a log home his father built by hand out of green pine for the total cost of $50, once stood within six miles of here. Ray and Myrtice had moved to the Cash Carter place when Crews was six months old. When they purchased the land, it was in bad shape, choked with weeds and lacking basic amenities like a mule lot, smokehouse, and tobacco barn. But Crews's parents hoped they could transform the plot into a farm that would support their growing young family. Subsistence farmers like Crews's father moved frequently, always in hopes that the next piece of land would be better, driven by the promise of a place where they could conjure enough income from the soil and buy a small measure of security. Crews's childhood was one move after another, spurred by a string of catastrophes both crop- and family-related. Crews could never point to a single house that contained his childhood, and it plagued him. The absence of a single home place, Crews wrote, was a "rotten spot at the center of my life." It made him feel anchorless, forever denied a place to moor his memories. Even here, in the place Crews identified with most strongly, claimed as his own, he never shook the sense of being an outsider. This feeling dogged him wherever he went, the conviction that he was doomed to be an interloper. It dripped, inevitably, into his fiction. After *Childhood* was published, an interviewer asked Crews why he wrote so often about alienated male characters. "I don't suppose you could imagine a more alienated human being than a South Georgia sharecropper who must move every year from one leeched-out patch of soil to another," Crews said. "Maybe if I write about alienated male characters, maybe this alienation comes just from my own life."

Crews stayed in a tenant house on the Cash Carter farm until the next disaster struck. His father worked from before sunrise until dusk, fifteen-hour days, clearing and planting and harvesting and hoping. One April morning after a hard winter, Ray Crews failed to rise at his habitual pre-dawn hour. He died in his sleep of a heart attack, "so massive and so sudden that he didn't move enough to wake his wife, who was sleeping with her head on his arm." He was thirty-one years old. His corpse was laid out on the front door of the house, as was the custom, but rather than having members of the family prepare his body for burial, Myrtice called in an embalmer. The expense of the embalmer and the coffin she bought from a funeral home in Waycross, at $60, was more than the sum cost of the house Crews was born in. Ray's body would be in a graveyard ten miles away, but when the embalmer drained Ray's blood, it was buried next to an oak tree near the house. The family dog, Sam, sat on the spot where the blood was buried for three days and howled. It was this oak that Haselden was looking for, tapping through the brush at the corner of the lot the trailer stood on. We fought through a mess of waist-high scrub toward the gnarled limbs of the only real candidate nearby, an oak with the bark scraped off in chunks toward the bottom of its trunk. "Here," Haselden said. We stopped and stood in silence for a couple of beats until the mosquitoes, swirling up from the damp ground, tormented us back into the truck.

WE CONTINUED ON, past the wreckage of the house where Crews and his mother had once fled his drunken father, and down the mud-encrusted road. Haselden paused the truck near a dirt path that cut its way through the pine trees, leading into the blue-black horizon. "There were three log houses down here, just shanties," Haselden said. One of those houses, Crews wrote, belonged to the family of his childhood best friend Willalee Bookatee, a black boy about the same age as Crews who used to come over and help spin his Sears Roebuck fantasies.

Crews devoted a good chunk of *Childhood* to Bookatee and his family. He sits down to a meal with them, relishing a supper of baked possum stuffed with sweet potatoes, served with fried and steamed okra. After they eat, Auntie shows Crews how to bury the possum's eyes in the back of the house to prevent the creature from looking for them in the afterlife. Bookatee is Crews's constant companion, and the butt of his pranks. "Willalee was our friend, my brother's and mine, but we sometimes used him like a toy," Crews recounted. "How many afternoons would have been endless if we couldn't have said to one another: 'Let's go get Willalee Bookatee and scare the shit out of him.'" (Bookatee gets back at Crews by filling an apple full of cow dung disguised with blackberry jam on top, convincing his friend that it's a homemade treat.) Crews named a character in *The Gospel Singer* after Willalee—in the book, a man named Willalee Bookatee Hull gets lynched for the rape and murder of white debutante named MaryBell Carter—and one in *A Feast of Snakes* after Willalee's sister Lottie Mae. In that book, Lottie Mae is the woman who butchers the one-legged sheriff's privates after he assaults her.

"Funny thing is," Haselden said as he peered down the path, "Willalee was fiction. Never was a little boy named Willalee Bookatee, not as far as we know. There were black people that lived here, but we never could remember Bookatee. Of course, that would have been before my time. This was the place here he was describing, but as far as we know . . ." Haselden shrugged.

None of the Crews scholars I spoke with had much of a lead on a real-life Bookatee. When I consulted Ted Geltner, he noted that Crews didn't make any reference to Bookatee in his letters, though Haselden's sister Eugenia mentioned Bookatee being one of the children playing pop the whip when Crews was flung into the boiler. (Crews's other nonfiction pieces contained the occasional embellishment, but Geltner believes that *Childhood* doesn't, more or less.) Erik Bledsoe, who edited several books about Crews, asked Crews about Bookatee in an interview, wondering why a close friend was the namesake of the character who met such an untimely end in *The Gospel Singer.* "He hemmed and hawed and said that he didn't realize he had done that," Bledsoe wrote in an e-mail. "I think he made him up. Or at best he's a composite. But I don't have any evidence either way."

It's possible that Haselden and his siblings just didn't remember a little black boy who played with their sickly cousin, that he had escaped the net of family myth. No doubt there was enough to worry about without taking notice of which neighbors Crews was keeping company with when he recovered. Bookatee could have simply faded away, replaced with more pressing matters of sick children or sick animals, the never-ending cycle of crops, keeping people fed and clothed. Yet it seems unlikely that a figure that loomed so large in Crews's young life escaped the attention of his kinfolk, that some story of Crews and Bookatee's mischief wouldn't have been banked in the vaults of treasured anecdotes passed on. Haselden could trace the outline of a wraparound porch from a house demolished more than fifty years ago, and recall the year that the road up to his house had been paved. If Bookatee had been around, or another Bacon County resident who fit his description, I doubt Haselden and his siblings would have forgotten him. These are not people who handle family history casually.

But it would also be odd for Crews to have inserted such a large piece of fiction into his memoir. Crews approached *Childhood* as a project of radical honesty, an exorcism of the nightmares he had lived through as a young boy. He had hoped committing his ordeals to the page would be a catharsis, a way of ridding himself of the ghosts of Bacon County. Instead, the agonies of his childhood burrowed still deeper. Writing the book nearly killed Crews. After *Childhood* was published in 1978, Crews descended deeper into alcohol and drugs, a period he told interviewers was exacerbated by the psychic trauma of digging through his past. "I was writing about people who had lived and many of whom are still alive, including my mother," Crews told an interviewer from *New Letters* in 1989. "Many of the facts were terribly unlovely—worse than that, ugly—and I didn't want to unnecessarily pain any of those people. That book hurt me the worst. It burnt me bad. I have never been quite right since I wrote that book."

Recounting the facts of his life in Bacon County was so tough because it denied Crews the comforts of fiction, the usual distances he allowed through the imagination. If Crews did invent Bookatee, it might have been a small valve for the tremendous pressure he had put on himself to get Bacon County right. Rereading

Childhood, I found clues that Bookatee might be fiction rather than flesh, an imaginary companion who helped Crews through his trials. One passage in particular seemed like a knowing wink from Crews:

> Since where we lived and how we lived was almost hermetically sealed from everything and everybody else, fabrication became a way of life. Making up stories, it seems to me now, was not only a way for us to understand the way we lived but a defense against it. . . . And Willalee Bookatee and his family were always there with me in those first tentative steps.

A sign? Bookatee's people—were they another Bacon County family or the denizens of Crews's head, nourished by the time he spent in bed with his department-store catalogs? But then, clues are much easier to find once you think you have the solution to the puzzle.

I don't think it matters. Bookatee, imaginary or not, was a function of Crews's honesty, not a deviation from it. If he is a fabrication, he's one Crews drew in service of the larger truth he was working to convey. Like the stories that Crews heard from his relatives about the father he never knew, the tale can't be severed from the teller. It is real because we believe it to be, because we accept that Crews wrote with the intention of telling a story larger than the details it contains. "What apprentices don't understand is the important thing is not the fuck-

122 | SOUTH TOWARD HOME

ing story," Crews said to one interviewer. "The important thing . . . is the writer's vision of the world. It doesn't matter what he writes about. My writing will have a certain taste and a certain smell and a certain sound."

Crews's years living in Bacon County were some of his most difficult, but they were also the ones that he kept circling back to in his writing. The ongoing crises of his time there never dampened his attachment: When Crews died in 2012, he left instructions for his ashes to be scattered on Hurricane Creek, so strong was the pull of his first home. His aim was to tell about the place he grew up, and the people he grew up with, in the fullest, most accurate way he could.

6. Harper Lee and Truman Capote's Courthouse
MONROEVILLE, AL

On the spectrum of Southern writers, Harper Lee and Harry Crews are about as far away from each other as you can get. Crews's following is small but fervent; his books are beloved but not widely circulated. Harper Lee wrote a novel that vaunted her to an excruciating level of worldwide fame; her work still inspires Halloween costumes and celebrity baby-name choices. Crews's writing is harsh and absurd where Lee's is gentle and mischievous; he writes about the rural and blue-collar where she addresses life among the middle class in Monroeville—a six-hour drive west of Bacon County. But both focused their life's work on documenting the innards of a home place, grappling with the ways that Southerners try to preserve their traditions while overcoming entrenched racial inequality. Either one could have uttered Scout Finch's famous assessment: "I think there's just one kind of folks. Folks."

THE DRIVE THROUGH the rural Alabama roads toward the sleepy town of Monroeville, the hometown of Harper Lee and the inspiration for her most famous creation, *To Kill a Mockingbird*, is a quiet one. No interstates come near that hilly patch of rural southwest Alabama. If you're hoping to get gas, grab a Twinkie, or go to the bathroom, you had better stop off in Selma on your way, because the approach to Monroeville didn't have so much as a run-down Chevron to offer. For miles around, there were little more than pastures full of cows, great gleaming catfish ponds, abandoned gas stations, and hulking, mute crosses. The AM radio stations offered only crackling static, interrupted by snippets of sermon. I had set out for Monroeville at a predawn hour, and as I drove, trails of dusty pink began to streak through the gray winter sky. As I wound farther south down the country roads, Spanish moss began gathering on the trees and hawks glared down from telephone wires. My traveling companion was a dear friend of mine named Sarah, a whip-smart Alabamian with close ties in Monroeville; as we drove we gossiped about Alabama politics and the newest construction projects in Birmingham. I asked Sarah to come along for company because she knew the little town backward and forward, and because she had talked about paying a visit to her family friends down there the last time we spoke. One of those friends was Harper Lee.

The visit I made was months before the bombshell news that, fifty-five years after *To Kill a Mockingbird* appeared, Lee was publishing a sequel of sorts to her bestseller. The new book, called *Go Set a Watchman*, had been written before *Mockingbird* but deals with the same characters. With the announcement, reporters descended on quiet Monroeville, and my trip, though I didn't know it at the time, was in the calm before this storm.

But I didn't meet Harper Lee in Monroeville. Of course I didn't: She was, and is, famously averse to inquiries from the press, flatly turning away journalists who fly from New York or Los Angeles to knock on her door just as surely as those who drive down from Birmingham or up from Mobile. She stopped giving interviews about fifty years ago, and speaks to reporters rarely and briefly, maintaining a tightlipped-ness that would have inspired the envy of Calvin Coolidge. A rejection slip from Lee may be as much a point of pride for reporters as those from *The Paris Review* and *The New Yorker* are for fiction writers.

Lee is vigilant about her privacy. Her image in the media is that of a shadowy recluse, the J. D. Salinger of southwest Alabama. In fact, Lee is just quiet. She has a reputation for being generous and friendly to the few whom she takes under her wing, far from the cantankerous spirit that many a rebuffed reporter has painted of her in the press. Her celebrity combined with her talent for keeping out of the papers has infused her appearances with an extra element of magic.

But even though I knew how unlikely it would be to meet Lee, I still half expected for her to show up, maybe drinking coffee at a booth in the local McDonald's or taking a walk through the square. She seems to have a sense of whimsy about revealing her presence, like a local god or mythical sprite. Lee has been known to eschew formal, celebrity-filled engagements but show up at a library's summer reading program festival or a local high school production of *To Kill a Mockingbird*. Lee might appear at a symposium for writers or at your Easter dinner table, invited by a friend of a friend. Local authors who sent copies of their novels to Lee's house in blind hope have sometimes gotten handwritten notes of encouragement. My father, a doctor at the University of Alabama for many years, once received a signed copy of *To Kill a Mockingbird* from a grateful patient who was one of Lee's Monroeville neighbors. Growing up two hundred miles away in Birmingham, I was always aware that Lee had not only touched all of our lives with her writing, she could show up in person when you least expect it.

Lee had suffered a stroke in 2007, which meant that she was less mobile than before. Previously, she had split the year between living in New York City and Monroeville. Sarah had sometimes squired Lee around New York in those years, and it always gave me great pleasure to imagine her and Lee flying under the radar somewhere on the Upper West Side, ordering a cup of coffee from a bodega, traipsing through Central Park, or window-shopping along Fifth Avenue just under the noses of the journalists who would write perennial think pieces about Lee's disappearance from public life. In New York, Lee sometimes attended dinner parties for stray Alabamians and friends. One of the times I missed meeting her was there, at a potluck supper hosted by an acquaintance. By all accounts she was sharp-witted and sweet-toothed, unpretentious and welcoming to fellow Southern stragglers who by stroke of luck had been seated next to her.

Lee's declining health had confined her recent activities to Monroeville more or less, though she still appeared at the Presidential Medal of Freedom ceremony, posing for pictures next to George W. Bush, the Texan commander-in-chief towering over her slight frame. In recent years, reports had drifted up from Monroeville that Lee was becoming increasingly withdrawn and wary. She had stopped signing copies of her book, once such a common occurrence that, as a schoolchild on a field trip to Monroeville, I remember a teacher submitting a list of names to one of Lee's friends for her to inscribe copies of *Mockingbird*.

She had even landed in the news for filing a suit against the Monroe County Heritage Museum, demanding they cease selling souvenirs based on *Mockingbird*. The museum, the most prominent feature of the tiny town of Monroeville, is essentially a monument to Lee and her book. The courtroom of the museum hosted regular re-creations of the famous scene in *Mockingbird* where Atticus Finch addresses the jury over the fate of Tom Robinson.

The case settled out of court, but some Monroeville citizens commented to the press that the case felt like an attack on the hometown that had nourished and celebrated her fiction. It was, in fact, the result of a long-simmering tension between Lee and her hometown's efforts to either celebrate or capitalize on her fame, depending on one's point of view. Monroeville, in the meantime, was changing. Lingerie company Vanity Fair, which had opened operations near Monroeville in the 1930s and been the major employer in the area for years, had only a handful of its once robust workforce. The nearby paper mill shut down in 2009, laying off all of its employees, the machinery sold for scrap. Once the manufacturers fled, Monroeville doubled down on its fame as the "Literary Capital of Alabama," drawing about 20,000 tourists a year to a city that, by the last census count, has only around 6,500 residents. As New York City has the Village, Monroeville has the Book.

Yet Monroeville residents are fiercely and famously protective of Lee. More than one out-of-towner from a well-respected news outlet has been unwittingly guided right past Lee as she sat at a corner table. Only a few Monroeville natives seem to be outside of an unspoken policy of silence, and they pop up over and over again in Lee-related articles: George Thomas Jones, who once worked as a caddy for Lee's father, is one, and Reverend Thomas Butts, the pastor of the Methodist church in Monroeville, is another. A highly vaunted "interview" with the *Daily Mail* on the fiftieth anniversary of *Mockingbird* consisted of Lee thanking the reporter and saying, "We are just going to feed the ducks but call me the next time you are here. We have a lot of history here. You will enjoy it." Translated from Southern politesse, that gracious dismissal might be rendered as "Don't let the door hit you on your way out."

THE CENTERPIECE OF *To Kill a Mockingbird* is the lone architectural landmark of Monroeville: the county courthouse. The courthouse square sits at the center of town and is really the only way that you would know that you had entered Monroeville. The opening pages of *Mockingbird* describe Monroeville's downtown, loosely disguised as the hamlet of Maycomb, as it was in the 1930s:

> In rainy weather the streets grew to red slop; grass grew on the sidewalks, the courthouse sagged in the square . . . bony mules hitched to Hoover carts flicked flies in the sweltering shade of the live oaks on the square. Men's stiff collars wilted by nine in the morning. Ladies bathed before noon, after their three-o'clock naps, and by nightfall were like soft teacakes with frostings of sweat and talcum.

By the time *Mockingbird* came out, the court square had lost some of the leaky-molasses pace that Lee described in her book. Gone were the mules, and even the live oaks. When art director Henry Bumstead, tasked with adapting the quiet town of Maycomb to the screen for the film version of *Mockingbird*, came to Monroeville

in 1962, his crew found the square too modernized to
use for their exterior shots. No mules, no Hoover carts.
(They ended up re-creating much of Monroeville on a
back lot in Hollywood, including a painstaking replica
of the inside of the courthouse.)

Today, the square is the liveliest place in town.
Monroeville remains, as Lee wrote about Maycomb,
"an island in a patchwork sea of cotton fields and tim-
berland," a government town in the countryside of
southwest Alabama prevented from much growth by
its location far away from the closest ports. Around
the courthouse, a perimeter of faded brick buildings
keep guard. Chipped, faded signs advertise long out-
of-business dry-goods companies, but the occupants of
the buildings are mostly banks, county offices, and boutiques specializing in monogrammed canvas totes and
college football team–themed hair ribbons. The corner hardware store, now out of business, was once the
town's all-purpose shopping stop; couples would register for their weddings there. Outside the store stood
large birdhouses painted with references to *Mockingbird* and the square; nearby is Radley's Fountain Grill,
named after Lee's fictional shut-in, Boo, and the Maycomb Mall. The offices of Barnett, Bugg, Lee & Carter,
where Harper Lee's father, Amasa Coleman Lee, and
sister Alice Finch Lee both practiced, is a block away.

The museum itself is a small one, mostly run by volunteers. Three years after the publication of *Mockingbird*, county employees moved out of the building and

into the offices scattered around the square. In 1968, still riding the wave of Lee's publication fame, the courthouse reopened as a local attraction.

The first floor has the gift shop and a small exhibit about the history of Monroeville, which began, like so many Alabama towns, as an agricultural crossroads for exporters of timber and cotton. One room is devoted to a re-creation of a country lawyer's office, a nod to Lee's description of the nook Atticus Finch worked out of in the courthouse early in his career, though the room is crowded with leather-bound books—a far cry from Lee's description of a room that only contained "a hat rack, a spittoon, a checkerboard, and an unsullied Code of Alabama."

Lee's father, who went by A. C., was the model for the determined Atticus Finch and his virtuous if doomed quest to defend a black man from an unfair verdict in Depression-era Alabama. The match between Atticus and A.C. is, of course, not exact, but Lee noted in a 1962 interview with *The New York Herald Tribune* that they are alike "in character and—the South has a good word for this—in 'disposition.'" Like Atticus, A. C. was a well-respected presence in his small town. Along with his legal work, A. C. Lee was an editor of the *Monroe Journal* and a member of the Alabama House of Representatives.

"It is and it isn't autobiographical," Lee told the *Tribune* about her book. "For instance, there is not an incident in it that is factual. The trial, and the rape charge that brings on the trial, is made up out of a composite of such cases and charges. . . . What I did present as exactly as I could were the clime and tone, as I remember, of the town in which I lived. From childhood on, I did sit in the courtroom watching my father argue cases and talk to juries."

The courtroom, without doubt, is the centerpiece of the museum. A fair chunk of the $2.5 million that was poured into renovating the courthouse, correcting the "sagging" part of Lee's description, was used to shine up the old courtroom, preserving the setting of the fictional trial in *Mockingbird*. The film version of the book had re-created the airy room exactly, a detail that Monroeville residents often recount with pride. Its on-camera doppelgänger and the carefully preserved 1930s details—hard, pewlike wooden benches, tin jugs balanced on the tables once occupied by the plaintiff and opposing counsel, a wide balcony encircling half the room—conspire to give the room the quality of a film set. In fact, it is a set of sorts. The courtroom's main role in Monroeville life is as the fulcrum of the annual *To Kill a Mockingbird* play, one of the town's major yearly tourist attractions. The court scene is often reenacted here for tour groups, with sullen-looking middleschoolers acting as the jurors. The play migrates from inside the courthouse to the open square, where a row of re-created shotgun shacks acts as a stand-in for the street where Scout Finch and Boo Radley live.

"The Play" is as ubiquitous a term in Monroeville

as "the Book." In the weeks leading up to the six-week series of performances, it is the main focus of the town. The cast is made up of local volunteers, many of whom have returned to play their roles for years. In recent years, the production values of the play have escalated, as has the attention paid to the players. The outdoor cottages, once working sets taken down after the play's run, are now permanent fixtures. The play traveled to Hong Kong in 2012 as part of a cultural exchange. Nelle Harper Lee has reportedly never come to see it.

On the day Sarah and I visited, the courtroom was being used as an auditorium for a heritage festival. Women in richly patterned head wraps watched children doing a dance routine in front of the judge's bench. On the balcony, where Sarah and I ascended to observe the proceedings, groups of grade-school children craned their necks over the railings to watch their friends, occupying the same place that Lee and Scout Finch had during trials held here.

The courthouse's transformation into a sanctuary for Lee's novel is an amusing turn of events considering the unflattering, if affectionate, way she described the building in *Mockingbird*. The Maycomb County Courthouse is a mélange of architectural styles, where "Greek revival columns clashed with a big nineteenth-century clock tower housing a rusty unreliable instrument, a view indicating a people determined to preserve every physical scrap of the past."

That preservation is still in full effect. It's the familiar paradox of small Southern towns: The only way to move on from the past is to embrace it. One of the ways that Monroe County has pivoted away from the ravages of industrial collapse is to re-create a work of literature that records one of its worst chapters. History and a sense of chagrin about its unfolding are the only resources the South has ad infinitum. *Mockingbird* is, at its heart, a book about the begrudging evolution of Southern mores and manners. Mid-Depression Maycomb is a place stuck by both circumstances and design in the mire of the past, where the future holds less appeal than the potential buried, still glimmering, in years behind them. It is as if, by faithfully re-creating their history, the residents can by some voodoo conjure back the imagined glories of the antebellum era. Racial equality, the old and poisoned logic goes, is an affront because it breaks with the way things have always been, no matter the way they should be. *Mockingbird* is beloved by middle-schoolers across the country for its clear message about the value of the fight for social justice. Atticus Finch may have lost his case defending the black Tom Robinson from the Jim Crow legal system, but there's no question that his quest is a virtuous one. Even the young Scout Finch manages to accidentally diffuse a KKK-flavored mob outside of the courthouse that has vaguely violent intentions toward her father.

When Lee published her book in 1960, Alabama was deep in the turmoil of the lead-up to the civil rights movement. It was 1964 when the Civil Rights Act was passed, and 1965 when nearby Selma briefly became the most infamous place in Alabama for the bloody face-off between police and protestors. Publishing a thinly veiled account of her small Alabama town's grappling with deeply entrenched racial divide was a bold declaration. It was an act of protest that shone the national spotlight on Monroeville. Even with the obvious tenderness Lee has for her hometown, her portrait risked alienating great swaths of the community that she grew up in. In her lifetime, she has seen Monroeville, ouroboros-like, advance in the only way it knows how, moving away from the past by making more of it to emulate.

Outside the entrance to the courtroom is a wizened piece of trunk encased in glass with tiny, old-timey toys scattered around its base. THIS, proclaims a plaque, IS THE FAMOUS TREE. It is, to the best of anyone's reckoning in Monroeville, a live oak that stood between Lee's childhood home on South Alabama Avenue and the Boleware place, where a shut-in named Son, who may have inspired the character of Boo Radley, lived. There's no real evidence that Boo Radley was more than loosely based on Alfred "Son" Boleware, a local recluse whose reluctance to leave the house made him a similar object of speculation for local kids. But the Boleware place has passed from local legend into the larger network of literary myths surrounding *Mockingbird*. Even the pieces of the book that are taken wholesale from Lee's imagination seem to find physical vessels, much to Lee's apparent amusement. At an awards ceremony for an essay contest in 2006, Lee told a reporter that one girl came up to her and informed her that Boo Radley lived across the street from her grandparents. "Well, I didn't know what to say to that," Lee replied with a laugh.

The tree that the chunk of lumber outside of the courtroom represents has become one of the book's main symbols, often incorporated in the design for the cover of the book. In *Mockingbird*, Boo leaves little gifts for Scout and her brother, Jem, in the knothole of a similar live oak. In the final chapters of the book, the "malevolent phantom," as Lee describes him, saves Scout and Jem from a vengeful Bob Ewell, bent on punishing Atticus for the humiliation he wrought on him in the courtroom by attacking his children. "Boo was our neighbor," Lee writes. "He gave us two soap dolls, a broken watch and chain, a pair of good-luck pennies, and our lives."

It is an irony lost on no critic or would-be biographer of Lee's that the press now treats her as Scout and Jem once treated Boo Radley. Among the many standard tropes in an article about Lee (including some variation of "To _____ a Mockingbird" in the title, making reference to Monroeville's access to Walmart, describing a failed attempt to contact Lee) is comparing the author to the spectral presence of Radley. Lee seems to encourage the comparison, even though it exaggerates her reclusiveness, perhaps also in an attempt to hammer home the moral that Scout and Jem learn at the end of the book, that the kindest thing you can do for some people is to leave them alone. According to Mary McDonagh Murphy's *Scout, Atticus & Boo*, when Oprah Winfrey attempted to convince Lee to appear on her show for the fiftieth anniversary of *Mockingbird*'s publication, Lee declined by citing Radley's character. "If you know Boo," Lee reportedly told Winfrey, "then you understand why I wouldn't be doing an interview, because I am really Boo."

On either side of the tree are a series of small rooms, places that Lee described as "sundry sunless county cubbyholes . . . hutches that smelled of decaying record books mingled with old damp cement and stale urine." With its conversion into a museum, the court-house replaced the musty old spaces with airy rooms lined with blown-up historical images of Monroeville, quotes from Lee's limited interviews typed across them in 90-point font.

A good portion of the exhibit is devoted to the making of the Oscar-winning *Mockingbird* movie, particularly the time that Gregory Peck came to scope out the small Alabama town he was representing on camera. The movie was also a turning point in the town's conception of *Mockingbird*, from a local footnote to a coun-trywide sensation. People in Monroeville alive to see Peck's visit still trade stories about seeking out his auto-graph or spotting him as he strode across the town square. In photos, Lee seems as swept up in the excite-ment of the Hollywood star's visit as anyone else. She escorted him around town, introducing him to her curious neighbors, showing him the courthouse square. Many of the stock images of Lee are from that visit, particularly one in which Lee and Peck are eating at the Wee Diner, Peck turned toward Lee as she holds a cigarette in one hand and looks deep in thought.

Lee's experience with Hollywood was apparently a uniformly positive one. Unlike other authors who chafe at seeing their work adapted to the silver screen, Lee seemed genuinely pleased with the end result. She championed the screenplay, written by Horton Foote, as a work of art. In the liner notes to the movie's DVD release, Lee praised Peck's interpretation of Finch. "When he played Atticus Finch, he had played himself, and time has told all of us something more: when he played himself, he touched the world," Lee wrote. Lee and Peck became fast friends after his role. Peck told interviewers later that Lee was so moved by his performance in the movie that she gave Peck her late father's gold pocket watch. When Peck died in 2003, Lee traveled to attend his funeral. Her support of the movie has never wavered. "I think it is one of the best translations of a book to film ever made," Lee said to the *New York Times* in 2006. It's the only adaptation that Lee has ever given her blessing.

Noticeably absent from the rooms dedicated to Lee are any actual artifacts of her life in Monroeville. There is mention of Lee's family: her sisters, Louise and Alice;

her father, A. C., and his similarities to Atticus. There is the note that Lee's name is her aunt Ellen's, spelled backwards. (She decided on her middle name, Harper, for her books because she didn't relish the thought of accidentally being called "Nellie.") There are statistics about the global success of *Mockingbird*, the many languages it has been translated into and the many millions of copies sold. There are no personal treasures on display, no real comment from Lee that hasn't been culled from a national magazine. No objects in the room indicate that Lee lives within walking distance of the place. It is a visual reminder that the museum must, as every Lee fan and biographer, tread an impossible line, both attempting to satisfy widespread curiosity about Lee's life and attempting to protect her wish for privacy.

THE DEARTH OF information on Harper Lee's personal life is particularly striking when compared to the rooms dedicated to Monroeville's other literary sensation: Truman Capote, born Truman Streckfus Persons. Capote grew up spending his summers with his cousins, the Faulks, who lived next door to Lee. The Faulk family had donated a slew of artifacts from Capote's youth to the museum after the writer's death in 1984. There are handwritten letters between Capote and his aunt Mary Ida Faulk, as well as pages from a family photo album and a colorful, worn crocheted baby blanket he rarely traveled without, even as an adult. The notes from Capote are lively and tinged with family gossip. In one, he derides his estranged father's attempt to trade on Capote's fame as part of his business selling penny scales. In another, he explains having to delay a visit back to the South with fellow Alabamian, actress Tallulah Bankhead. "I honestly think it would be a mistake for us to stay right in your house," Capote writes. "Tallulah stays up all night every night and never gets up till five in the afternoon."

Capote and Lee's childhood friendship worked its way into both writers' fiction. A version of Lee appears in Capote's first novel, *Other Voices, Other Rooms,* as the sassy, tomboyish Idabel Thompkins. In *Mockingbird,* Capote is the model for Charles Baker "Dill" Harris, the slightly effeminate out-of-towner who eggs on Scout and Finch's investigation of the Radley house. "Dill was a curiosity," Lee wrote. "He wore blue linen shorts that buttoned to his shirt, his hair was snow white and stuck to his head like duck-fluff; he was a year my senior but I towered over him."

Lee could have been describing—and indeed might have been—the oddly formal childhood photo of young Capote, blown up and hung on one of the walls in the museum. In it, Capote looks like a shrunken serious scholar, his hand deep in the pockets of his formal shorts, and a smile semisuppressed. Like Dill, Capote blew in as the summer began, got into mischief, and left again in the fall. Like Dill, Capote's worldliness was partially earned and partially faked, a tumultuous family situation eased by an abundance of chattering Alabama cousins. Capote clearly identified with Lee's fictionalized version of himself, even going so far as to boast about it. "Nelle's book is high on the bestseller list," Capote wrote to his friends Alvin and Marie Dewey after *Mockingbird* came out. "And yes, my dear, I am Dill."

The relationship between attention-loving Capote and publicity-shy Lee has long passed into mythology. It's not unusual for a large city to birth several writers who enter the literary canon, but for a small rural town in the Deep South to do so is remarkable. They seemed like an Algonquin roundtable of South Alabama embodied in one friendship. Even standing in the sunlight-soaked rooms full of Capote's personal items, it's easy to envision them at parties, Capote at the center of the table and Lee making quick, dry jokes at the edge of the room.

Neither Lee's nor Capote's fictional depictions of each other garnered as much attention as their collaboration on *In Cold Blood*, Capote's much-lauded work of narrative nonfiction that became a touchstone of New Journalism. Capote, riveted by a 1959 *New York Times* item—just three hundred words long—about a massacred Kansas family, proposed a piece on the murders of the Clutter family to *The New Yorker*. He invited Lee to join him as a research assistant of sorts. At the time, Lee was deep in the process of *Mockingbird*'s publication. The manuscript had been accepted, but it would be several months before the book hit shelves. "She is a gifted woman, courageous, and with a warmth that instantly kindles most people, however suspicious or dour," Capote told George Plimpton in an interview. "Feeling at loose ends, she said she would accompany me."

During their time in Kansas, Lee joined Capote and took copious notes, about 150 pages in all. She provided an extra set of observations for Capote's research, but more than that, she helped oil the social interactions between the brash Capote and the Kansans he hoped to interview. Lee, speaking to *Newsweek*, cracked, "Those people had never seen anyone like Truman—he was like someone coming off the moon." Alvin Dewey, a detective in charge of the case who later became a friend of Capote's, described the two of them later in the *Garden City Telegram*: "If Capote came on as something of a shocker, she was there to absorb the shock. She has a down-home style, a friendly smile, and a knack for saying the right thing."

Capote echoed this assessment to Plimpton. "A Kansas paper said the other day that everyone was wonderfully cooperative because I was a famous writer," he said. "The fact of the matter is that not one single person in the town had ever heard of me." The two months that the writers spent in Kansas became the basis for a four-part serial that ran in *The New Yorker* in 1965, and eventually became *In Cold Blood*. Something about the idea of Lee and Capote conducting a murder investigation in a sleepy Kansas town has stuck in the literary imagination, the soon-to-be famous homespun novelist convincing churchgoers to have tea alongside a quirky, diminutive, flamboyant New York celebrity. Those few weeks became the basis of not one but two movies on Capote's life, *Capote* and *Infamous*. Catherine Keener and Sandra Bullock, respectively, play Lee. The fanfare around the movies drew another crop of would-be interviewers down to Monroeville, a development Lee, one imagines, was less than thrilled by.

The falling out between Capote and Lee is as mythologized as the relationship between them, though the details of their estrangement aren't as firm. Sometime after Lee's star ascended with the publication of *Mockingbird*, the two friends drifted apart. When *In Cold Blood* finally hit shelves, Lee was credited only as "assistant researchist," a title that didn't acknowledge the lengths to which she had gone to aid him in his work and how crucial her help had been to the project. No doubt Capote's acid tongue and the tightening grip of alcoholism played some role. In the years between *In Cold Blood*'s publication in 1966 and Capote's death from liver cancer coupled with drug intoxication in 1984, he became a regular on the talk-show circuit and an incorrigible gossip, recounting stories of his famous pals and their glitzy gatherings. Perhaps Lee didn't want to be another celebrity acquaintance mined for cocktail fodder. Certainly a comment that Capote made about Lee's mother did nothing to help matters. Frances

Finch, Capote said, had twice tried to drown Lee in the bathtub. "Both times she was saved by one of her older sisters," Capote told his biographer, Gerald Clarke. "When they talk about Southern grotesque, they're not kidding!"

Capote's sensational claim, posed so glibly, was then echoed by many articles on Lee, either as a way to explain her later reticence toward the press or as a provocation of sorts. It opened the door to the exact kind of attention that Lee goes to lengths to avoid, making her the target of tabloid speculation. Probes into Finch's nature revealed little but secondhand whispers about her mental health and stories about her fondness for crossword puzzles. Whether there is truth in it or not, it was clearly a betrayal of Lee's trust to air such a thing in a national setting. One repetition of the story drew the ire of Alice Lee, who until recently acted as her sister's liaison to the press. "It was a fabrication of a fabrication," Alice Lee told the Associated Press in 1997. "It is false. How would you feel if someone told a story that in essence accused your deceased mother of being an attempted murderer?"

Then there is the persistent conspiracy theory that Capote, not Lee, really wrote *Mockingbird*. Capote never discouraged rumors that gave him credit for the book publicly, though in a letter to his cousin Mary Ida in 1959 he says that he had seen the book and "liked it very much. She has real talent." Literary critic Pearl Belle, who possibly had been privy to some unsubstantiated commentary by Capote on the novel's success, floated the claim originally. No doubt part of the reason it took root so strongly in the public imagination is thanks to the one-hit-wonder nature of *Mockingbird*. But Capote's and Lee's literary styles, aside from being steeped in the dialect and mannerisms of a small south Alabama time, are not really that similar. The myth of Capote's authorship also smacks of sexism and a kind of privileged, New York–centric literary view. *How could this backwoods, publicity-shy woman write something so popular and profound*, it seems to say. *Surely we should look to her flashier male companion.* It is the kind of theory that seems aimed at punishing Lee for failing to play the game, for abandoning the salons and publishing lunches for her pocket of south Alabama. Lee has never commented publicly on the rumor, largely because she hasn't commented publicly on almost anything. It doesn't deserve the dignity of a response. But it must have rankled her to see her success attributed to Capote.

THERE ISN'T MUCH left at the intersection where the Lee family house once stood. Lee and her family moved away from South Alabama Avenue and the Faulk home when she was still young. The house is gone, but a crumbled back fence that once separated the two backyards remains. The little section of South Alabama Avenue where Lee grew up is just a couple blocks north from the courthouse square, easy walking distance for *Mock-*

ingbird tourists. The Lee family moved away from the spot in the early 1950s, after Lee's mother and brother died unexpectedly in the same year. At the site of the old Lee house is a Mel's Dairy Dream, planted there after the Lee house was razed and before *Mockingbird* fever took hold of the town. The Faulk house is gone too. In its stead is a historic marker with a microbiography of Capote and his time in Monroeville, staid camellia bushes dotting the property. Lee has resisted the town's attempts to place her own marker there, or to rename South Alabama Avenue after her or her book.

Standing there, it wasn't *Mockingbird* that first came to mind—though this place is clearly the model for the house Scout lives in with her father and brother—but Capote's short story "A Christmas Memory," a gorgeous, tender tale of preparing for the holidays with his cousin Sook. Sook, who called Capote "Buddy," was the one who made the baby blanket that was in the museum. (There is a *Citizen Kane*–esque story about Capote's last words being "It's me, it's Buddy," perhaps addressed to a vision he had of his cousin.) "It's always the same," Capote wrote. "A morning arrives in November, and my friend, as though officially inaugurating the Christmas time of year that exhilarates her imagination and fuels the blaze of her heart announces, 'It's fruitcake weather!'"

At my Alabama high school, it was an annual tradition for our gregarious principal, once an acquaintance of Capote's, to read aloud "A Christmas Memory." It's easy to see why it was so warmly embraced: It's a story that shows the best of Southerners, a kindhearted elderly woman and her six-year-old ward saving their pennies to bake fruitcakes for near-strangers, a ritual of quirky generosity that jibes with a certain fondness for weirdos that the South nurtures. It offers the reader a direct line to Capote's heart, to one of the relationships most precious to him, cutting through the thick crust of persona he built in his later years. And, like *Mockingbird*, it is a part of a South rarely written about, the region between the julep-swilling porch dwellers in Faulkner and the country folk of Crews and O'Connor and the Jim Crow terrorized black community in Richard Wright and Zora Neale Hurston. It is about the middle class.

In *Mockingbird*, Scout and Jem exist in a state of relative indifference toward money, one afforded them by their father's stature and steady job. "There was no hurry, for there was nowhere to go, nothing to buy and no money to buy it with, nothing to see outside the boundaries of Maycomb County," Lee writes. Much of Scout's education in *Mockingbird* comes from running up against the race and class prejudices woven into the fabric of Maycomb's social life, being forced to understand the way the social categories of the small town she lives in amplify or diminish hardship. These realizations dawn on her slowly, and Lee often relays them to us with a heavy hand. There is the scene when Scout informs her teacher that her classmate, Walter Cunningham, can't afford to buy lunch. His family, like many poor Southerners, bartered what they had for services, a fact Scout explains clumsily to the slick Yankee import Miss Caroline: "Walter hasn't got a quarter at home to bring you and you can't use any stovewood." The Finch family's housekeeper, Calpurnia, later scolds Scout for her tactlessness, for though Scout has grasped the class differences between her and the Cunninghams, she hasn't figured out the subtleties of pride and poverty.

There is no talking about *Mockingbird* without addressing race. The central story of the book is about the deeply entrenched racial injustice that Atticus Finch seeks to help correct through his defense of Tom Robinson. The lessons in it are not difficult to grasp. Atticus presents his nuggets of wisdom like deep-fried Zen koans: "The one thing that doesn't abide by majority rule is a person's conscience" and "You never really understand a person until you consider things from their point of view . . . until you climb into his skin and walk a mile in it."

Critics of *Mockingbird* often sneer at Lee's approach to these issues as lacking in nuance, absent of any moral ambivalence. "It's interesting that all the folks that are buying it don't know they are buying a children's book," Flannery O'Connor sniped. But *Mockingbird* faithfully follows O'Connor's own guidelines for how best to shake an audience out of complacency: For the hard of hearing, you shout. Lee spells out the uncontestable rightness of racial equality in terms that a fifth-grader could understand. If *Mockingbird* sometimes reads as cartoonish, it is only because the essential message of Robinson's trial is one that now seems glaringly evident. *Mockingbird* has elements of a caricature, a sly message about grown men failing to acknowledge truths that a child of Scout's age can clearly discern. It does the book a discredit not to acknowledge how skillfully Lee made a then radical-sounding conclusion about civil rights sound so obvious, so palatable that her book is now a staple of middle-school curricula.

At its heart, *Mockingbird* is about manners. It is an attempt to catalogue them but also to gauge their value, to determine which codes of honor are worth following and which deserve to be challenged. In one of her last formal interviews in 1964, Lee made this goal explicit. "As you know, the South is still made up of thousands of tiny towns," Lee said. "There is a very definite social pattern in these towns that fascinates me. . . . I would simply like to put down all I know about this because I believe there is something universal in this little world, something decent to be said for it, and something to lament in its passing. In other words, all I want to be is the Jane Austen of south Alabama."

The Jane Austen line may have been half-joking, but it's also revealing. *Mockingbird* is a novel of sensibility. Lee's work elevated the social struggles and scandals and injustices of a tiny town into something of wider interest. It is not a gothic tale; it is a radio drama. It is the weight that Lee afforded these small incidents that makes her book remarkable, a declaration that the quotidian affairs of a nowhere town deep in the Bible Belt were both relevant and worth preserving.

———

SARAH AND I stopped for lunch at David's Catfish House, a restaurant just outside the town center, where Lee and her sister used to come for lunch. It was a faux log cabin, filled with long wooden tables set with condiments and rolls of paper towels. The house specialty was fried catfish and hush puppies, those dollops of fried cornbread that, legend has it, were used in the Civil War to quiet the yaps of Confederate dogs. Lee's sister preferred to order their catfish cooked "continental"— broiled with spices—and order the children's plate, while Lee herself would opt for a traditional helping of the breaded, crispy fish. I ordered the same, along with a slice of buttermilk pie. In the kiosk outside, a headline on the *Mobile Register* blared news about Lee settling with the museum.

After lunch, Sarah, armed with some potted plants and cookies, took us to the assisted-care home where Miss Alice Lee, a friend of Sarah's family, lived, in order to pay her a visit. In years past, if a journalist wanted to talk to Lee, the best bet was to approach her sister. For years the sisters lived together in an unassuming brick house near the town elementary school, a home so cluttered with books and papers it was said that you could, on occasion, find a volume in the oven. Alice Lee served as her sister's intermediary, lawyer, and press representative. A slight, sharp woman whom friends called Miss Alice, Lee's sister worked as a lawyer in her father's office until after her hundredth birthday, making her the oldest practicing attorney in the state before medical problems forced her into retirement. She died some months after our visit to Monroeville at the age of 103, and the remembrances, like most profiles of Miss Alice, focused on her mental alacrity—in order to stay sharp, she recited the presidents, vice presidents, and secretaries of state in order every night before bedtime—but equally remarkable was her wry humor. When Alice Lee was asked by the *Birmingham News* her secret to longevity, she responded, "I don't do anything to bring on dying."

A stamp of approval from Alice Lee functioned as a tacit nod from Nelle. You can hear Alice's voice in almost any project about the book that Nelle didn't overtly object to, though she rarely granted interviews about anything other than her law practice. (One such exception is director Mary Murphy's documentary *Hey, Boo*, which captures Miss Alice's lively, gravelly voice in all its glory.) Much of the difficulties between Monroeville and Lee were exacerbated by this system breaking down.

Inside the nursing home where Alice Lee lived, a gracious nurse in Garfield-printed scrubs let us into a waiting room, where Miss Alice's diploma from law school hung alongside a photo of her and Nelle, grinning, at a luncheon. But Alice, in fragile health, wasn't up for seeing visitors. We left the plant, cookies, and a note on the sideboard already cluttered with Valentine's Day presents.

Before we headed out of town, Sarah had another plant to drop off, at the nursing facility where Harper Lee lives. And that was when a sort of anxiety set into my stomach, at the ludicrously small chance that, despite all evidence to the contrary, maybe Lee would be curious about Sarah's friends, invite me in, want to have some tea. If you're a fan of her work, the prospect of meeting Harper Lee poses a conflict, since it is so well known that she has no particular wish to meet her adoring public.

And the gap between the mythology of a writer and the realities of the writer's life is wide, of course. Because she keeps so private, that's particularly true in Lee's case. It reminded me of a pilgrimage Harry Crews went on to talk to one of his favorite writers, Frank Slaughter. He hitchhiked to see Slaughter and rang him up, only to find him occupied at the barbershop. "The notion that a writer had to get a haircut! I mean, writers don't get haircuts. They don't have to deal with everything the rest of us do, do they?" Crews told an interviewer. "I just couldn't put together my own love of literature— the mystery, the overwhelming, profound grandness of literature—with going to the barbershop and getting your hair cut." It's a disappointment that's completely unfair, that flies in the face of every hard-earned lesson about all people just being the weak, interesting, complicated beings that we all are, but it exists nonetheless, that your heroes still have to get haircuts instead of living on a plane of existence where they can avoid every human inconvenience. Harper Lee could never live up to the idea I had of Harper Lee.

Sarah drove us to the assisted-care home where Lee lives. On the way, we stopped at the Dollar General, where I made a quick, frantic hunt for some suitable item to bring to Lee as a gift, some small token that could bear the weight of all the hopes and well wishes and tidings I hoped to convey. Such a talisman, unsurprisingly, proved impossible to find. And I knew, even at the time, that the search was a ridiculous one. It wasn't just that the Dollar General was piled with coloring books, canned goods, discount makeup, and cheap cat collars—not exactly the fare of a thoughtful visiting gift. It was that talismans are basically meaningless except to the holder. I could mentally inscribe whatever message I wanted onto, say, a box of chocolates and all Lee would see is a snack. There was no secret code, no riddle to be unlocked. I settled on a chocolate Easter bunny, one of those pastel-festooned numbers with a single, unblinking eye peering out from the packaging. It would have to do.

I followed Sarah into the foyer of the cheery facility. Unlike most of the buildings around Monroeville, there was no sign of anything *Mockingbird*-related: No painted birdhouses, no murals, no hint of the famous resident in their midst. As I watched Sarah walk up the hall and disappear into a room, I thought of the things I wanted to say to Lee.

That I was a fan, obviously. That she and I had people in common. That I hoped the winter weather hadn't been too hard on Monroeville and I hoped her bingo games had been paying out for her. That I, too, had gone to New York City as a wide-eyed Alabama girl, hoping to write something true about the South, to convey some small part about the place I grew up, its fiery strangeness and treasures and tangled past. That I understood how impossible that mission was, but felt it was the only thing worth doing.

I kept thinking about an encounter that the journalist Michael Clarkson had with J. D. Salinger in the 1970s. Clarkson knocked on Salinger's door to try to coax the author out for a drink, to perhaps lure him into giving an interview. Salinger refused, but he also rebuffed Clarkson in a way that's always haunted me, that pointed to the clash between writers as mythological figures and writers as people. "I have no obligations beyond my writing. I have nothing to answer for," Salinger said. "You're just another guy who comes up here like all the rest and wants answers, and I have no answers." And that, essentially, would be what I would be if I met Lee: just another visitor who treated her like an oracle instead of a person, demanding answers that she didn't have for questions I couldn't articulate.

After a few minutes, Sarah walked back down the

hall. Lee was asleep, anyway. Before we left, I had Sarah leave the chocolate bunny for her, just inside her door. On the box, I scribbled a note. It read: "Dear Nelle, Sorry to miss you. Thank you for everything. With admiration, Margaret."

7. John Kennedy Toole's Hot-Dog Carts
NEW ORLEANS, LA

Culturally, John Kennedy Toole's South is closer to Harper Lee's than the distance between them might indicate. South Alabama towns like Monroeville have more in common with New Orleans than other places in the state. An hour and a half's drive south from Monroeville will land you in Mobile, home of the oldest Mardi Gras celebration in the country, founded some fifteen years before the parties in New Orleans. In that part of Alabama, jambalaya is as much a part of tradition as biscuits and moon pies. If you drive along the Gulf Coast, down from Monroeville through Mobile, you can make it to New Orleans in a little over three hours.

JOHN KENNEDY TOOLE was thirty-one years old when he pulled his blue Chevy Chevelle onto a road shaded by pine trees outside of Biloxi, Mississippi, strung a green garden hose from the exhaust pipe into the back left window, locked the car, started the engine, and slowly asphyxiated himself on the poisonous cloud of carbon monoxide pumping in. Two months earlier, he had walked out on his job as a professor at Dominican College in New Orleans and skipped town abruptly after a nasty spat with his mother. The inside of the car, the deputy sheriff who discovered Toole's body reported, was spotless, Toole's hair neatly combed, his clothes pressed and clean. In his pocket, his mother later told interviewers, was a stub proving that one of the last stops on his journey had been to Flannery O'Connor's house in Milledgeville, Georgia. On the passenger seat, Toole had balanced a ten-inch stack of letters, papers, and notebooks on top of a black suitcase, topped by a final note to his family. What papers from this pile Toole's mother did not get rid of were impounded by the Biloxi Police Department, and then destroyed by the floodwaters of Hurricane Camille. In Toole's back room in New Orleans was a box containing the manuscript for the novel he had struggled over for six years, *A Confederacy of Dunces.*

The story of how *A Confederacy of Dunces* went from a collection of smeared onionskin pages in a bedroom in Uptown New Orleans to a Pulitzer Prize–winning comic novel published eleven years after Toole's suicide has become as integral to the book's identity as its sputtering, bombastic main character Ignatius J. Reilly. It is as marvelously unlikely as the plot of the book itself, as the city of New Orleans in which *Confederacy* is set.

After Toole's death, his mother, Thelma Toole, applied herself with relentless vigor to getting her only son's manuscript published. Thelma was a stubborn woman with a penchant for drama. In later interviews, John Kennedy Toole's friends described Thelma as a type who landed somewhere in the spectrum between "stage mom" and "micromanaging parent," though one went straight for "megalomaniac." She had raised her son with a care that teetered on the edge of obsession. (One of the composition books Toole had left behind had "Mom, please don't touch" written on the cover, echoing Ignatius Reilly's Big Chief notebooks scrawled with "MOTHER DO NOT READ.") She worked as an elocution expert, coaxing students out of their thick New Orleanian accents, and was fond of rolling her *r*'s in conversation, often sporting opera gloves despite the thick swamp heat of southern Louisiana. She lobbed the increasingly tattered pages of the manuscript at publishing houses. Eight houses turned her down; the financial risk of a comic novel by a deceased author unable to promote, edit, or otherwise help the work presumably outweighed its literary merits, and editors were no doubt put off by Thelma Toole's impatient, repeated letters. "Each time I sent it off first class and it came back bulk rate," she later told an interviewer.

Finally, in the fall 1976, Thelma spotted a line in the *Times-Picayune* about novelist Walker Percy, who had immortalized his own corner of New Orleans in *The Moviegoer*, who was teaching a writing seminar at Loyola University for one semester. Thelma began pestering Percy with phone calls, entreaties to read the manuscript that Percy gently rejected. But one day after Thanksgiving, Thelma, outfitted in a pillbox hat and a thin layer of talcum powder, traveled over to Loyola with her elderly brother Arthur disguised as her chauffeur. She intercepted Percy as he was leaving his evening class, presenting him with a white box containing the torn pages of Toole's manuscript.

"Over the years I have become very good at getting out of things I don't want to do," Percy later wrote in the introduction to *Confederacy*. "And if ever there was something I didn't want to do, this was surely it: to deal with the mother of a dead novelist, and, worst of all, to have to read a manuscript that she said was *great*, and that, as it turned out, was a badly smeared, scarcely readable carbon."

But Percy, out of some combination of politeness, surprise, and sympathy, took the manuscript that Toole offered, drove home, and read it. In mid-December, Percy sent Thelma a letter full of admiration for the book. "[Toole has] an uncanny ear for New Orleans speech and a sharp eye for place," Percy wrote. "I don't know any novel which has captured the peculiar flavor of New Orleans neighborhoods nearly so well." Percy committed to help usher *Confederacy* into print, using his literary clout and connections to move it out of the slush pile. Eventually, Louisiana State University Press published the tome in 1980, editing very little from the stack of smudged onionskin pages that Thelma had pushed on Percy. Buoyed by the unusual circumstances behind its publication—a triangle between a dead author, an eccentric mother, and a National Book Award winner made excellent copy—*Confederacy* got the attention of reviewers and climbed up the bestseller lists. In 1981, the book won the Pulitzer Prize for Fiction, cementing its ascent from near-garbage to literary gem.

THELMA TOOLE, by all accounts, had prepared for fame her whole life and spent much of Toole's childhood priming him for greatness. When the fame at last arrived, rewarding her grief and toil, she was not humble about it. Thelma assembled an entourage of friends to squire her about town, introducing herself as "mother of the scholarly and literary genius John Kennedy Toole." She gave to her friends as gifts relics from her son's life: a pair of his nail clippers, a set of his worn bed sheets. NBC flew Thelma to New York for an interview with late-night host Tom Snyder, in which she asserted her role as a medium to bring her son's talent into the world. "I walk in the world for my son," Thelma concluded, a line that became her mantra.

When interviewed, Thelma used the opportunity to lambast the publishing industry for her many rejections, particularly focusing her ire on storied editor Robert Gottlieb, who had corresponded with Toole about *Confederacy* in the early 1960s. The letters that exist between Gottlieb and Toole are full of encouragement and suggestions for revising *Confederacy*, though Gottlieb thought the novel needed substantial work before it could be published. Nevertheless Thelma used her new platform to excoriate Gottlieb, not so subtly implying that the editor was responsible for the decline in mental health that drove her son to suicide. "Gottlieb is the villain," Thelma told *People.* To a reporter at *Horizon* magazine, she went on an anti-Semitic screed about Gottlieb, decrying him as a "Jewish creature . . . not a man."

Thelma took her tales of her son around New Orleans in a one-woman show, combining impressions of the characters in *Confederacy* with off-key musical numbers and stories about its author. In a video recorded at her home on Elysian Fields Avenue in 1983, Thelma, resplendent in a long rope of pearls and a lacy blue housedress, performs at a baby grand, a huge velvet curtain with "THELMA" lopsidedly emblazoned on it hanging behind her. The walls are crowded with pictures of her son and posters of *Confederacy*-related celebrations. "I produced a genius," Thelma boasts. "He had the seeing eye and the hearing ear."

Named Queen Mother of one of the Mardi Gras krewes, the social organizations that organize the annual festival parades, Thelma was infuriated when Walker Percy declined to come to her house for a knighting ceremony. To aspiring authors, Thelma's persistence became an aspirational tale, and to New Orleanians, Thelma became a celebrity, another character in the ever-evolving carnival of the city. When she died in 1984, just four years after the book's publication, her funeral drew a crowd of well wishers. When her son's body had been laid to rest in the family tomb fifteen years earlier, only three people were in attendance: his two parents and his childhood nanny.

The hoopla Thelma created, ostensibly in celebration of her son's talents, served to propel the book into publishing mythology but also muted the voice of its author. Toole could never contribute to the conversation, not just—and most obviously—because he died before his book entered the public sphere, but also because Thelma did her best to exert control over the narrative of his life. Thelma's vision of her son was of a long-suffering genius, superior in every way, a dutiful son driven to his death by the cruelties of the publishing industry. It's hard to read Thelma's account without wishing for a different filter, one less tinted by love and longing. Very few of us are as good as our mothers want us to be. But her clipped and trimmed version of Toole's days was the one widely disseminated, the voices of Toole's friends and coworkers relatively quiet in comparison. Several of Toole's closest confidantes, put off by the media hubbub over *Confederacy*'s publication, refused to speak about their late friend, taking whatever knowledge they had of Toole to the grave rather than join the frenzy.

Despite the dutiful work of scholars, the story of Toole's life is full of gaps that have been unconvincingly smoothed out, a biographical comb-over. There aren't many details of his final years, the ones in which he tangled with the stuff of his novel and ultimately abandoned it. We know only the barest outlines of what Toole was suffering from in the years before his suicide, stories that he told friends about the government implanting a device in his brain and someone stealing his manuscript and publishing it under another name. There's also not much information about Toole's romantic life. Toole's early biographers, René Pol Nevils and Deborah George Hardy, speculated that Toole's personal life was riddled with problems. In their account, *Ignatius Rising*, they trot forth theories that Toole was an alcoholic, tortured by questions about his sexual orientation, a gay and closeted artist unable to cope with rejection. They interviewed a man who claimed Toole owned a boardinghouse where a secret harem of gay men lived, feeding the author's promiscuous nature. This double life, they posit, may account for Toole's scathing representation of the New Orleanian gay community in *Confederacy*, for those Freudian notes in Ignatius's obsession with hot dogs. Toole's surviving friends dismissed the book as full of sensationalism and gossip from unvetted sources that Toole was not around to refute. Cory MacLauchlin, in his Toole biography *Butterfly in the Typewriter*, debunked many of their claims. "It is tempting to fit Toole into the trope of a fatally troubled artist, his genius unrecognized, sinking into an abyss of vices," MacLauchlin wrote. "The narrative is so commonplace that we seem willing to overlook a lack of evidence to believe it."

There's no way to tell. Thelma, who steadfastly refused to give permission to would-be biographers until her death, preferred not to talk about the final years of Toole's life. It's not surprising: What grieving mother wouldn't want to remember her son in his happier days, trussed up in costume for a Mardi Gras ball or grinning at the beach, rather than his fraught last years, plagued with anxiety and depression? The biographer's goals and the family's are often at odds. But Thelma's efforts to edit the documentation she kept later frustrated scholars' attempts to piece together a more complete version of Toole's life. Her archival methods followed her own rationale. She kept Toole's high school math homework, but there are no letters between him and his father. She destroyed Toole's suicide letter but kept her own perfectly preserved dental bridge.

People search for hints of Toole's voice because they wish there were more of it. His writing is so loud and theatrical that it makes his silence even more conspicuous. *A Confederacy of Dunces* is a book that's both brilliant and flawed, a romp through New Orleans so interesting that you barely mind the tour guide making fun of your shoes. Toole's portraits of New Orleanians seem like they were spoken to you surreptitiously while sitting next to him on a bench, taking in the crowd. You can't help but wonder what he would have written next. But Toole completists have only *Confederacy* and the considerably lesser *Neon Bible*, a novel Toole wrote when he was sixteen about a priest in Mississippi, published in the wake of *Confederacy*'s success. That, and we have New Orleans.

CONFEDERACY IS A BOOK about that most unlikely of cities as much as of any of its characters, the home Ignatius compliments as "the comfortable metropolis which has a certain apathy and stagnation which I find inoffensive." New Orleans is an easy place to write about, and a hard place to write about well. In popular culture, it's a giant kooky sports bar constantly beset by tropical storms or a swamp dotted with antebellum houses where men in seersucker suits ignore consonants and sip frosty juleps in their alligator-riddled backyards. It's a double-decker bus tour of the places leveled by Katrina. It's all fan boats and "Who Dat" and jambalaya, or it's poverty and failures of government and high-velocity winds. There is little account of the place between Bourbon Street and the Lower Ninth Ward.

I've been using one excuse or another to visit New Orleans my whole life, drawn down by the delights of fresh, powdery beignets and a slow trickle of friends into the city. In Jackson, where my parents live, people sometimes brag about making the three-hour trek down just for a nice Friday-night dinner. The directions to get there from Mississippi are simple: Follow the highway until the swamp eats it. Eventually, the ground drops out beneath the road entirely. You stop passing notices for counties and begin seeing ones for parishes; the squat warehouses filled with wholesale Mardi Gras spangles multiply; and finally the brackish expanse of Lake Pontchartrain stretches out languidly below, the shimmer of the Central Business District emerging on the horizon.

Going to New Orleans after a fresh reading of *Confederacy* gives the whole place a different flavor. I felt like a conspiracy theorist. Every sign began to read like a knowing wink, every passerby an excised extra from the book. As I drove in this time, pondering the eccentricities of Ignatius Reilly, I noticed a brewery sign recently rehabbed and installed on an apartment complex; its red neon letters blared FALSTAFF at the cars scurrying down I-10. (The letters, I later learned, change colors according to the weather report of the day. Green means fair weather, red is for an overcast day, flashing red and white means that a storm is approaching.) I read the sign as a bit of marginalia, a reminder of Ignatius Reilly's roots in the long-winded Shakespearean figure. New Orleans scrolled out before me like a manuscript marked up with a sure hand, a play with the director's notes scribbled in every street.

Toole was a native New Orleanian; his Irish-Creole background traced back to Jean-François Ducoing, a friend of the French pirate Jean Lafitte who earned praise from Andrew Jackson for his role in the Battle of New Orleans. (Thelma often went by her full name, Thelma Ducoing Toole.) Though he spent several years studying in New York, most of Toole's life spread from Uptown, one of the oldest, most well-to-do parts of New Orleans. *A Confederacy of Dunces*, Toole told his friends when he was working on the manuscript, attempted to convey the texture of the place, in all its whirling, over-lapping glory. "Irene, Reilly, Mancuso—these people say something about New Orleans," Toole wrote in one letter to Robert Gottlieb. "They're real as individuals and also as representative of a book . . . with Ignatius as my agent, my New Orleans experiences began to fit in, one after the other, and then I was simply observing and not inventing." It is the last phrase that struck me the most: *observing and not inventing*. That observational quality is one of the most compelling, purely fun things about *Confederacy*: It feels like an inventive friend taking you in confidence about the people in his office, or at her family reunion, mimicking their reactions and playing up their tics. If some fiction works by bringing the characters suffocatingly close, *Confederacy* works by keeping them all at arm's length. The joy of *Confederacy* is in its skill for recognizing absurdity in the familiar. It is a people-watching book, a taxonomy of the species of New Orleans.

Faulkner's New Orleans is a messy watercolor of a place, overrunning with pigment. Tennessee Williams's New Orleans is steamy, haunted, and claus-trophobic, full of nervous creatures and dilapidated boardinghouses; it always seems to be dusk there. The New Orleans that Toole paints in *Confederacy* is a different city altogether, the only place out of the three that I recognize. His New Orleans is wider, weirder, always on the move. It expands into the neighborhoods upriver, tracing the intersection of an oafish intellectual and his long-suffering henna-haired mother with a foul-mouthed Italian woman; a defeated policeman; a working-class con artist; a Bible-thumping geriatric; a crusading New York beatnik; and an underpaid, sarcastic black man who wears sunglasses indoors. Toole's characters don't speak; they scream. City life is a constant series of tiny social conflicts and misunderstandings.

In *Confederacy*, Toole pins down the fleeting, spontaneous communities that form in New Orleans. Round the right street corner, and you're suddenly swept up into a parade or a brawl or a funeral. You run into the same stranger repeatedly; you begin to suspect that you're simply waiting in the wings to be introduced into a story, that any minute you could be bound together with an unlikely companion. At the beginning of *Confederacy*, most of the characters are unacquainted with one another. By the end of the book, their lives are hopelessly snarled together. *Confederacy* is a chain reaction of coincidences coaxed into a pattern larger and more inevitable, something like fate. Its conceit is that it is about nothing, about the many nothings of ordinary life that somehow arrange, symphony-like, into the whole of everything.

New Orleans can read as a land of inexplicable quirks. The foibles of the city are numerous and well documented: here bodies are buried aboveground, and the seasons are, so goes the old joke, Summer, Hurricane, Christmas, and Mardi Gras. The sun rises over the West Bank. During the weeks of Carnival, emergency rooms teem with injuries suffered from overenthusiastic revelers whipping beads at breakneck speeds. Even trying to read a map in New Orleans is a translation exercise, the mixture of Spanish, French, and Louisiana English commingling in unruly collisions of syllables. In Toole's hands, the entropy makes sense, seems necessary. There is a code to the chaos, dream logic. *Confederacy* is often hailed for its grasp of the language of New Orleans, the flavors of dialect that Toole aptly mixed into the book. But he managed more than that. New Orleans has a grammar to it, and Toole was its most fluent practitioner.

THE MOST OBVIOUS *Confederacy of Dunces* landmark in New Orleans is the statue of Ignatius J. Reilly, positioned outside the former D. H. Holmes department store on Canal Street. I headed there. In a town full of eye-catching things, the statue is not one. The D. H. Holmes is now the Hyatt French Quarter, the statue tucked underneath a voluminous purple awning. Directly above Ignatius's bronze head hangs a black-and-white clock that completes the scene from the book, though it looks out of place near the sleek hotel doors. On the column nearby, a plaque has part of the opening paragraph of *Confederacy*. Ignatius, resplendent in his signature green hunting cap with earflaps "stuck out on either side like turn signals indicating two directions at once," surveys his fellow New Orleanians:

> In the shadow under the green visor of the cap Ignatius J. Reilly's supercilious blue and yellow eyes looked down upon the other people waiting under the clock at the D. H. Holmes department store, studying the crowd of people for signs of bad taste in dress.

When Mardi Gras is in full swing, the city removes the statue to prevent the crowds from desecrating or stealing it. (The temporary absence prompted an investigation by NPR in 2012.) But as I stood there, no one paid attention to the slouched bronze figure. Tourists wielding acid-green, alien-shaped plastic cups full of frozen cocktails bubbled past, on their way to browse stores stuffed with ribald T-shirts, hot sauces, souvenir cups, and cured alligator heads. Shoppers marched down the block, loaded with plastic bags in primary colors. A cart on the corner of Canal and Bourbon Street seemed to exclusively sell things emblazoned with Bob Marley's face: T-shirts, hats, bags, flags, pins. It was easy to imagine Ignatius tallying the offenses of passersby, the myriad violations against his moral standard of "theology and geometry."

Sculptor William Ludwig, who completed the Ignatius bronze in 1996, based the figure on John "Spud" McConnell, a local character actor famous for playing Ignatius in stage adaptations of *Confederacy*. The likeness is a fair one: There is the crumb-dotted mustache above a half smirk, the rumpled clothes, the shopping bag presumably filled with replacement lute strings, and the slumped posture of Toole's description. But as with every book character that looms so brightly in the imagination, it's an inexact translation into flesh or bronze. On Yelp!, where the statue has its own profile (and a four-and-a-half-star rating), fans who recognized Ignatius complained that he isn't quite right. "Docking a star because haughtiness level is just not high enough, the artist seemed to put a glimmer of compassion on his face" one reviewer wrote. "He can use 80 pounds of heft also."

True, Ignatius's statue seemed slighter than the mammoth-bellied figure Toole described. This bronze figure did not look like the man who, when perched upon a stool, "looked like an eggplant balanced on a thumbtack," who, as he waits for his mother fidgeting "sent waves of flesh rippling beneath the tweed and flannel, waves that broke upon buttons and seams." But the criticism is a tribute to how powerful a character Toole created. Ignatius is the critic incarnate, so it's little wonder some of his attitude gets reflected back on his own statue. He is a high-minded buffoon, overeducated and underexperienced, constantly aghast at his fellow humans' failings. He is all knowledge and no wisdom; nevertheless, his perspective is addictive. People become surreal cartoons, collections of flaws and eccentricities. While writing the book on his army base in Puerto Rico, Toole explained to Gottlieb in a letter, Ignatius began to hijack his thoughts. "In the unreality of my Puerto Rican experience, this book became more real to me than what was happening around me; I was beginning to talk and act like Ignatius."

It's not just Toole. Once you read Ignatius, you absorb him. You begin hearing his voice in your head, that sneering indignation at the oddity and incompetence of other human beings. When I first read *Confederacy* in high school, I found Ignatius merely amusing. When I read *Confederacy* after college, I recognized him. I began to see him everywhere. I saw a little of him in everyone I met, and in myself especially.

Toole created Ignatius in the 1960s, but there is a timeless quality to his cantankerousness. You can picture him being unhappy with any decade. He serves perfectly as a cartoon of an entitled twentysomething millennial. He still lives at home with his mother, Irene, after a lengthy period at college, where he studied medieval literature and philosophy and gained no practical skills. He is a relentless consumer—of hot dogs, of Big Chief writing tablets, of Dr. Nut soda—and produces only various kinds of hot air. He strictly reads obscure philosophers and Batman comics. Ignatius is the great-granddaddy of snark. He watches movies so he can confirm that he hates them. He lives to document violations against "good taste and decency." He feels these infractions bodily, through the function of his oft-mentioned "pyloric valve." For Ignatius, taste is an ethical code. A movie he dislikes isn't just a dud, it's a moral failure. The contrast between Ignatius's rigid rules for everyone else and his lax ones for himself is the source of several of the book's funniest scenes, like when Patrolman Mancuso visits Ignatius and Irene Reilly's tiny house in the midst of Ignatius's ranting at an *American Bandstand*–like television program that showcases talented kids:

> "I would like very much to know what the Found-ing Fathers would say if they could see the chil-dren being debauched to further the cause of Clearasil. However, I always suspected democracy would come to this." He painstakingly poured the milk into his Shirley Temple mug. "A firm rule must be imposed upon our nation before it destroys itself. The United States needs some theology and geometry, some taste and decency. I suspect that we are teetering on the edge of an abyss."

In a different era, Ignatius would have been terrific at the Internet. You can picture him tucked into his Constantinople Street bedroom with an empty case of root beer at his feet, crouched over a grungy, glowing laptop, posting screeds to his blog, adding pointed and overwrought comments below news articles. "When my brain begins to reel from my literary labors, I make the occasional cheese dip," Ignatius tells Patrolman Mancuso when asked about his profession, a statement that could also serve perfectly as a Twitter bio.

Toole's inspiration for Ignatius was medieval scholar Robert Byrne, a friend of his from a year he spent teaching at Southwestern Louisiana Institute, two hours west of New Orleans. Byrne taught at the tiny English Department of the institute, now the University of Louisiana at Lafayette, and shared an office with Toole. Like Ignatius, Byrne was a hefty, mustached fellow obsessed with the philosopher Boethius and his treatise, *The Consolation of Philosophy*, a tome that he assigned to every class he taught. The phrase "geometry and theology" was one that his colleagues recall Byrne using often, usually because one thing or another lacked in those qualities. Like Ignatius, Byrne loved hot dogs, wore a hunting cap with the earflaps arranged at odd angles, and saw no sense in clothes that matched. In his memoir *Ken and Thelma*, fellow faculty member and friend Joel Fletcher remembers Byrne appearing at the office one day in "three different kinds of plaid and an absurd hat." Toole, who was fastidious in his dressing habits, was taken aback, and told Byrne that he looked "like the April Fool cover of *Esquire*."

Anecdotes about Byrne paint him as a perfect Ignatian character. Fletcher writes about a time he was whistling while walking across campus with Byrne, who demanded to know the tune. Fletcher replied that he thought it was a Beethoven quartet's *scherzo*. " 'I've always resented *scherzi*,' said Bobby. 'They replaced the minuet, you know.' " A version of this exchange, which Fletcher likely relayed to Toole, appears in *Confederacy* when Ignatius asks if a hot-dog vendor is whistling a composition from Scarlatti. The vendor replied that the tune is "Turkey in the Straw," and Ignatius seems miffed. "I had hoped you might be familiar with Scarlatti's work. He was the last of the musicians . . . with your apparent musical bent, you might apply yourself to something worthwhile." Byrne even had the perfect response for interviewers who asked about his reaction after the success of *Confederacy*. When one reporter from the *Washington Star* asked if Byrne was bothered by his fictional likeness, you can practically hear the sneer in his voice from the reply: "I never read bestsellers."

Though Byrne's sartorial sense and verbal tics filled in the physical details of Ignatius, the character Toole created isn't just a caricature of an old friend, it's also a skewering bit of self-parody. For all his idiosyncrasies, Byrne was a successful teacher, content to live in a cottage near the school and practice medieval music in Lafayette. Ignatius lives at home, locked in a combative relationship with his mother, a description that much better fits Toole than Byrne. Nor were Ignatius's money problems alien to Toole: after the tightening grip of mental illness left Toole's father unable to support himself and Thelma, Toole kept his parents afloat financially. Ignatius reads as much as a compilation of Toole's greatest fears as a sketch of a real person. Ignatius and Toole are not the same, but his character acts as a conduit for Toole's observations about himself, and a fun-house mirror version of an academic with aspirations that don't match his circumstances. In Ignatius, he could express the worst of himself. "The book is not autobiography; neither is it altogether an invention," Toole wrote to Gottlieb. "I am not in the book; I've never pretended to be. But I am writing about things that I know, and in recounting these, it's difficult not to *feel* them."

From the spot below the clock at the former D. H. Holmes department store, Ignatius and his mother, Irene, round the corner to Bourbon Street to recover from a scrape with the law in a seedy bar called Night of Joy, a place that becomes a fulcrum of the freewheeling misadventures to follow. No such establishment exists, at least not exactly, but from the vantage point of the Reilly statue, you can see the spangled marquee sign for a jewel-box theater on Canal Street. The name of the establishment is "Joy Theatre" but the sign reads simply JOY in bold red letters, as if it were not a suggestion of feeling but a commandment for one. The theater was built in 1947, well in time for Toole to have taken note

of the blaring letters hovering on the horizon. I took it
as another note in the margins of the city and rounded
the corner.

IF YOU WERE blindfolded and dropped into the French
Quarter, it's possible that you could find your way onto
Bourbon Street just by your nose. Despite the vigilance
of the brave men and women of the New Orleans Sanita-
tion Department, the most populated blocks of the
street always smell like sugar and stomach acid. It was
late afternoon, and the night's rumpus had yet to begin.
Evidence of the previous night's partying clotted on the
sidewalks. Fleur-de-lis confetti, tiny plastic animals used
in cocktails, and feathers dotted the gutters of the side
streets, as if a horde of drunken, costumed Hansels and
Gretels were hoping to find their way back again. Every
other door leads to a glass-fronted daiquiri counter,
touting an electric palette of frozen, saccharine cocktails, served from constantly whirling machines into
huge Styrofoam cups. Groups of tourists in matching
colorful T-shirts floated from doorway to doorway like
schools of tropical fish. Above, on wrought-iron balco-
nies, bored-looking men in football jerseys held fistfuls
of cheap beads, waiting for an adequate target. At one
corner, a group of equally bored-looking evangelicals
held signs asking passersby about their relationship with
Jesus. It was, in short, excellent people watching. As
Ignatius says when his mother tries to pry him loose

from their place at Night of Joy: "We must stay to watch the corruption. It's already beginning to set in."

Confederacy is in part a satire of Bourbon Street. It's unlikely that any of the places I walked by literally had an act with a faux Southern belle being undressed by a cockatoo, but an animal act didn't seem farfetched, nor did a scheming owner with a policy of watering down the drinks. The exaggerated Southern-ness that Darlene can't quite nail in her act is a big selling point on Bourbon Street. "Come on in, y'all," a man beckoned to me, pointing to a sign for "The Swamp Thing," a mechanical bull painted green. "Laissez those bon temps right here."

As I stood tucked into the sidewalk, scribbling notes, an older woman with a perfect blond bouffant and frosted pink lipstick began speaking at me through a headpiece microphone. She wore a name tag that read MARION LIGHTFOOT and a khaki shirt. "Where you from?" she asked, pursing her lips. I began to explain my *Confederacy* mission and she cut me off. "Well, that's fine, but I'm going to have to issue you a ticket." She squinted at a saffron-colored notebook and checked off several offenses before handing me the slip with a flourish. The ticket had a tiny ClipArt illustration of an upset policeman under the banner "Party Pooper Award." My infractions included "Not Partying Hard Enough" and "Being Too Serious," as well as "Guy/Girl Watching" and "Being Too Good Looking." When I looked up, she offered a khaki visor from her bag with BOURBON STREET embroidered on the front and began to solicit a donation for a charity organization. "No thanks," I said, finally catching on. Her smile contracted. "Just hold this, cupcake," she snapped. "It's part of the skit." I complied. She finished her spiel and then whipped around to begin the script again. "Where you from? Wichita?" I heard as I scuttled away down Bourbon Street.

In my haste to escape, I almost missed the next stop on my Ignatius tour. There was no address for this one, but I had been assured that it would not be difficult to find, particularly along the tourist corridor parts of the city. I scanned the sidewalks for a distinctive red-and-white-striped uniform, feeling a bit like I had been plunged into *Where's Waldo?*. But finally, I spotted what I was looking for. There on the corner of Bourbon and Toulouse, sheltered under a bright red-and-white Coca-Cola umbrella, shone a seven-foot-long steel frankfurter with LUCKY DOGS emblazoned on top of the bun, and wheels attached to the bottom. A red attachment on top advertises the short menu: Lucky Dog, Regular Hot Dog, or Smoked Sausage. I had found a Lucky Dogs cart.

Lucky Dogs is a French Quarter fast-food staple, a beacon to those straggling home from the bars in search of sustenance or peckish while perusing the antique stores on Royal Street. It's the model for Paradise Vendors, the company that employs Ignatius as a lackluster hot-dog hawker in the second half of *Confederacy*. Lucky

Dogs has a lock on the New Orleans hot-dog market, thanks to a 1972 law that prevents pushcarts from operating in the Vieux Carré unless they had established themselves at least eight years prior. Lucky Dogs had been crawling through the Quarter since 1948, so the law effectively ensured a monopoly for the company. But the carts are more than a well-known stop for a five-minute dinner; they've also entered New Orleans iconography, thanks partly to *Confederacy*. Former Lucky Dogs manager Jerry Strahan wrote an amusing memoir of his twenty years employing a group of drunks, swindlers, misanthropes, and other outsized characters who worked as his hot-dog vendors; in honor of his famous fictional employee, Strahan titled the book *Managing Ignatius*. "Our crew is still made up of the same sorts of eccentric individuals that Toole must have met," Strahan writes in the introduction. "I had considered calling it 'A Hundred and One People I Wish I Had Never Met,' but I couldn't narrow down the list."

Painters in Jackson Square offer watercolors of the carts, and the company sells ties, visors, and Christmas ornaments emblazoned with the Lucky Dogs logo. Drinking stories about New Orleans often end with the apocryphal tale of some hooligan riding on top of the cart when the vendors push them back to the garage around four a.m. Some couples rent out the carts to cater their wedding receptions. (The minimum package for catering, three hundred hot dogs with all the fixings, starts at $747.) There is a Lucky Dogs stand at the airport, and one appeared briefly in Disneyland Paris. Even at the time Toole wrote *Confederacy* the carts were everywhere, and had a reputation for being manned by colorful characters, the sort who would rather not report to an office job. The one I stood in front of was doing brisk business despite the early hour, handing out wienies to a line of dudes in baseball caps and knock-off Oakleys. I got in line.

Confederacy might have bumped up the Lucky Dogs image, but it doesn't really celebrate the carts' gastronomic offerings. Ignatius gets hooked into selling wienies after he stumbles upon the cart garage and notices "the distinct odors of hot dog, mustard and lubricant." When Ignatius asks the ingredients of the meaty treats that "swished and lashed like artificially colored and magnified paramecia" in the pot of boiling water, his boss-to-be, Mr. Clyde, replies, "Rubber, cereal, tripe. Who knows? I wouldn't touch one of them myself." Not exactly appetizing, but it doesn't deter Ignatius. He eats four in a row after that.

Ignatius makes a miserable hot-dog salesman. He refuses to sell hot dogs to customers who violate his standard of geometry, eats most of his wares himself, and then lies to Clyde about being robbed. Instead of pushing the cart around well-trafficked areas, he parks out of the way and jots notes on Marco Polo. "The wagon is a terrible liability," Ignatius writes in his journal. "I feel like a hen sitting on a particularly large tin egg." He attempts to trap a stray cat and put her in the bun compartment of the cart to keep as a pet. He wheels it to a society ladies' art showing on Pirate's Alley—the narrow street behind St. Louis Cathedral where Faulkner once lived—to mock their paintings. During all these antics, Ignatius sports the vendor's uniform that "made him look like a dinosaur egg about to hatch," later jazzed up at Mr. Clyde's insistence with the addition of a plastic pirate's cutlass, a red sateen bandanna tied around the hunting cap, and a clip-on gold earring. He attaches a sign to the front of the cart that reads, in crayon, "TWELVE INCHES (12") OF PARADISE," which is inevitably vandalized with sketches of "a variety of genitals." He abandons the cart to go watch movies in the middle of the day and ultimately uses the wagon's warming compartment to smuggle pornography.

Toole had firsthand experience in the hot-dog-selling game. While studying at Tulane, he sold wienies at football games to earn an allowance. In *Ignatius Rising*, the authors cite a musician friend of Toole's, Sidney Snow, who used to push a Fiesta Hot Tamale cart around the French Quarter. Toole would take over Snow's route in a pinch. But even without years spent pushing around a wagon of wienies, it's easy to see why Toole would choose that occupation for Ignatius. It's a great vantage point for making observations about the city, as integral to New Orleans as the taxi driver is to New York City. It's the perfect spot at the edge of the ceaseless parade.

I stood in line watching the vendor spear the pink

sausages and present them to customers on pillowy buns, smothered in chili and relish and cheese. He used the universal utensil of the hot-dog vendor, the telescoping two-pronged tiny fork, the same kind Ignatius uses to flip dogs out of boiling water, and the same kind that his manager used to threaten Ignatius's Adam's apple when the lumbering medievalist eats most of the day's profits. He was wearing the trademark red-and-white striped smock, topped by a lace-patterned fedora. He had gray, wispy hair and was missing his two front teeth. His name, I learned, was Jerry. I ordered a Lucky Dog with onions and asked if he had ever read *Confederacy*. "People ask me that all the time," he replied good-naturedly, squirting ketchup on the hot dog as he spoke. "But nope, I sure haven't. The library seems to always be out of copies." I paid him for the hot dog and furtively checked the bun compartment for porn or kittens. It harbored neither.

I HAD REACHED my Bourbon Street saturation point, so I moseyed off to my next stop, munching the hot dog happily. My destination was in the Bywater, a pleasant ways away from the clang and churn of the Quarter. On my way out of the Vieux Carré I swung by Napoleon House, once offered by the mayor of New Orleans to the French leader as a refuge, later a favorite spot for Toole to drink with his friends, and now a famous Creole restaurant. I walked down Pirate's Alley, where

Ignatius crashed that art show, past St. Louis Cathedral, where Patrolman Mancuso had sought shelter. Outside the cathedral, in the wide promenade that circles Jackson Square, another Lucky Dogs vendor pushed his cart past palm-readers, voodoo wannabes, and human statues. A sousaphone player entertained the line of people outside Café du Monde, where tables of people merrily sipped chicory coffee and ruined their clothes with clouds of powdered sugar wafting from hot beignets. I walked east past Frenchman Street, past a twenty-four-hour combination bar and Laundromat, past vintage stores that displayed enormous feathered Mardi Gras headdresses, past a man in a camper chair selling gumbo from a bubbling pot beside his feet. Music from brass bands curled around the corners, beckoning. Further east, into the Bywater, I ran into a rolling bank of fog and emerged outside the compound of folk artist Dr. Bob, whose paintings of cultural icons, decorated with bottle caps, instruct would-be visitors to "Be Nice or Leave" as well as "Who Dat or Leave." I turned up Dauphine Street and hit upon the Bywater Art Lofts.

The lofts are in the former J. H. Rutter Rex Manufacturing Building, the place Toole probably used as inspiration for the Levy Pants factory. Toole based his portrait of the slowly dying Levy Pants on his time working part-time for Haspel Brothers, a clothing company famous for its seersucker suits. (A paystub for a week's work, $40, is among the papers Thelma kept.) Toole worked there after graduating from Tulane at the age

of twenty, thanks to skipping two grades in elementary
school. His boss was the son-in-law of one of the Haspel
brothers, and no doubt some of his observations from
the situation later drifted into *Confederacy*'s description
of the hapless Mr. Levy and his exercise-board-addicted
wife. Before his stint as a hot-dog seller, Ignatius works
at Levy Pants briefly, until he gets fired for an attempt
to foment a revolution among the factory workers, a
campaign that he describes as a "Crusade for Moorish
Dignity." He charms the senile Miss Trixie with athletic
socks and lunch meat, throws away the filing he's supposed to do, and instead builds a detailed cross. Toole
describes the building as "two structures fused into
one macabre unit," a sickly thing in the corner of the
neighborhood. "Alongside the neat gray wharf sheds
that lined the river and canal across the railroad tracks,
Levy Pants huddles, a silent and smoky plea for urban
renewal."

Renewal had come, but not at the behest of any
smoky plea. The Bywater was one of the few neighborhoods left relatively intact after the devastation of
Katrina, part of the "sliver by the river" protected by
a natural levee. The sudden influx of people into the
neighborhood coupled with the lack of housing stock
made the once-abandoned factory look more appeal-
ing than Toole might have seen it. A group of investors
converted the space into apartments for lower-income
artists. The former factory, trimmed in primary colors, now had various watercolor projects stuck into the

windows to dry, giving it the appearance of an upscale elementary school. A few lanky men in T-shirts smoked cigarettes outside the door and spoke in low tones.

THE EPICENTER OF *Confederacy* is in the French Quarter, but except for this brief foray east, the rest of the book moves west up the crescent of the Mississippi River. Constantinople Street, where Toole places the ramshackle house in which Ignatius and his mother lived, is in Touro, in the Twelfth Ward, a streetcar ride away on the St. Charles line. Toole paints the area as a claustrophobic, working-class one, where you can hear your neighbors through the walls and humid nights draw people out onto their porches. It's the kind of place where nosy homebodies write anonymous letters to one another, sniping about untoward behavior. The Reilly home, Toole writes, was the tiniest one on a block of houses "that dripped carving and scrollwork, Boss Tweed suburban stereotypes separated by alleys so narrow that a yardstick could almost bridge them." The Reillys' yard is bare except for a frozen banana tree and a leaning cross built on the burial spot of the family dog, Rex.

I walked down Constantinople from St. Charles, down from the pine-green streetcars that undulated away from the avenue, past the wizened trees that filtered the watery sunlight. In *Confederacy*, Patrolman Mancuso "inhaled the moldy scent of the oaks and thought, in a romantic aside, that St. Charles Avenue must be the loveliest place on earth." Though Toole lived farther Uptown, I always thought of that line as a little love note to his home slipped among the pages. It's an easy sentiment to feel on a warm day, something about the rich arboreal aroma, the green-gold shade painting the sidewalk. On the corner of Magazine Street, a pop-up bakery was selling king cake, the scent of baking cinnamon-sugar dough wafting out from the ventilation system. Toward the river, on the southern blocks of Constantinople where the Reillys' home would have been, little shotgun houses in pastel colors lined the block like Easter eggs in their carton. In one of these, perhaps the one with slanted shutters and a striped awning, or the one with a crumpled front gate, Ignatius could have been upstairs bellowing "Big Girls Don't Cry" to the distress of his neighbors, Irene Reilly hiding her muscatel in the oven.

Constantinople Street had shifted since Toole had seen it last, weathered almost half a century, a storm, and an ensuing wave of construction. At first I couldn't figure out what bothered me about the difference between the place as it stands and the one in *Confederacy*. And then I realized: It's too quiet. No chatters or cackles leaked from the houses, no gossip or complaints echoed through the slim alleyways. What I was missing was the voices, the fretful "Al Smith Inflection" of Irene's y'at accent, that linguistic anomaly that appears simultaneously in deep New Orleans and deep Brooklyn. I had been straining my ears for Ignatius's bellows, Irene's sighs, the slangy endearments of her friend Santa Battaglia. Toole so deftly populated the street with their clamor that I had half expected to be able to eavesdrop on them.

Constantinople Street is not far from the Prytania Theatre, the movie temple Ignatius frequented to better understand the failings of Hollywood. Irene and Santa walked there through the fictional parish of St. Odo to see a Debbie Reynolds movie, through the summertime "cacophony of dropping pots, booming television sets, arguing voices, screaming children, and slamming doors." Ignatius was even conceived thanks to the Prytania, after Irene and Mr. Reilly had gone there on a date to see the Clark Gable romance *Red Dust*. "Poor Mr. Reilly," Toole wrote. "He had never gone to another movie as long as he lived." The Prytania Theatre of the 1960s was a neighborhood single-screen palace bedecked with a columned entrance and a grand marquee. The one that I visited was a squat, redbrick block with a blue cursive "Prytania" sign on the upper-right corner of the building, as if a giant had casually autographed the place. The lobby, a pamphlet under the box office assured, had recently undergone extensive renovations. Iced coffee was now available alongside the usual shrink-wrapped boxes of Sno-Caps and bags of buttered popcorn.

Ignatius visited the Prytania religiously to hate-watch whatever they offered, his paunch spilling out over the armrests, an array of snacks occupying the seat next to him. Toole was an avid moviegoer, and some element of Ignatius's behavior might have been culled from his own audience pet peeves. (Some, too, must have been self-parody. In *Butterfly in the Typewriter*, one friend remembers Toole interrupting a couple snickering at the folly of Southerners during a screening of *Birth of a Nation* in order to lecture them about the finer points of Reconstruction.) He paints Ignatius as the worst kind of movie watcher, the obnoxious scream-at-the-screen kind, the one who is quickest to remind you of the special effects and to spoil the ending. He examines the close-up faces of actors for scars and cavities, he yells in the kissing scenes about the probability of halitosis. In his journal, Ignatius proclaims that he seeks refuge there to ogle "Technicolored horrors, filmed abortions that were offenses against any criteria of taste and decency, reels and reels of perversion and blasphemy that stunned my disbelieving eyes, that shocked my virginal mind, and sealed my valve." But, of course, that's the joke. Ignatius isn't interested in the potential of the cinema as an art form; in fact, he shies away from one film he suspects might be good. He's there to bolster his world view by puncturing the illusions of other moviegoers, to confirm his rightness.

The punch line here is the same one in the book's title, which Toole took from Jonathan Swift: "When a true genius appears in the world, you may know him by this sign, that the dunces are all in confederacy against him." Ignatius sees nothing but stupidity around him; he thinks of himself as an infiltrator at the party, scoffing at the small talk. But to the reader, he's clearly just as much a participant in the confederacy as any of the other characters. The loftiness of his perspective is a farce. And as you snicker at Ignatius, you begin to suspect that your own perspective is equally skewed. *Confederacy* is a book about the impossibility of just watching. There's no such thing as an innocent onlooker, as someone who's just a member of the audience. It's a book that makes you conscious of life's general absurdity, the ridiculous things we do that pass for pragmatism. We are all confederates in the duncedom.

FROM THE PRYTANIA, I drove farther uptown to poke around the neighborhood in which Toole lived for most of his life. Thelma and Toole's father, John, a nervous car salesman, moved to the edge of the affluent neighborhood shortly after Toole was born. Thelma positioned the family there in order to enter into the competitive social games of high-society New Orleans, to distance herself from her downtown upbringing. The family moved from house to house, clinging to the neighborhood even when it was no longer financially practical. In later years, Toole paid his parents' rent on their Uptown apartments, setting aside a portion of his wages from the Army to prop up their place in the neighborhood. The last place he lived in New Orleans was there, a house on the corner of Hampson Street, not far from his job teaching at the all-girls Dominican College.

On my way to see it, the houses begin to widen and grow taller. The leafiness intensifies. The hues are muted creams, mossy greens, barely-there pinks, as if the neon colors of the French Quarter had washed, diluted, upriver. The house Toole lived in last is now sea-foam green with neat white trim, hemmed in by a row of hedges and a wrought-iron fence. A cheery flag with autumn leaves waves by the door. An attic window peers out from the roof like a periscope. Near the gate, a tasteful plaque marks the home as the Toole-Hecker House, in deference to the family that built the place in 1885 and its most famous tenants. At the corner outside of the house is where Toole had his final argument with Thelma before rocketing away in his car, destined eventually for that pecan grove outside of Biloxi.

Within the pages of *Confederacy*, it's easy to picture the Toole his friends described, the one who impressed girls with his dance skills and quaffed cocktails in the Roosevelt Hotel's Sazerac Bar, the gifted mimic and notorious cheapskate, the Marilyn Monroe obsessive and sharp dresser. It's harder to imagine him after the party was done. I couldn't conjure up the Toole who lived here, the dedicated teacher slowly unraveling in the stuffiness of his family home. Bobby Byrne, the model for Ignatius, described his friend as "extroverted and private," that most heady and paradoxical of combinations. He was a shapeshifter, as we all are. To his mother he was a doting genius, to his acquaintances a real card, to his readers an unsung literary hero. He even has different names to go with those different identities: "Ken" for his Louisiana friends, "John" for his New York buddies, "Kenny" to Thelma, and the full-bore "John Kennedy Toole" for the rest of us. Here, at the spot where Toole lived in his last days, was where I felt most acutely how little information there was about Toole's personal life. His warm, witty voice in *Confederacy* brings him so close that it's jarring to realize you know nothing about him, that you are strangers still.

My final stop was the point on the map farthest from the Ignatius statue, an outlier on the arc from the French Quarter to the Toole home Uptown. Toole's remains, once collected from his car in Biloxi, were interred in the Ducoing grave in Greenwood Cemetery, up the expressway toward Pontchartrain, near City Park. New Orleans is famous for its cemeteries, the deceased interred in aboveground vaults thanks to the high water table and Spanish tradition. They are popularly referred to as cities of the dead, thanks partially to a half-admiring, half-horrified observation Mark Twain made about their architecture in *Life on the Mississippi*. Greenwood Cemetery is a suburb of the dead. The graves are plotted in neat rows on streets named after flowers and fruit: Tulip, Evergreen, Lily, Magnolia, Lemon. A man on a riding lawnmower neatened the edges of the grassy avenues.

I went into the office of the funeral home for help with directions, and met a father-son pair of undertakers. A brochure on the father's desk showed the cemetery's monument to the Fireman's Charitable Association, and, in bold, "Always Prestigious, Still Affordable." I told him about my mission and he brought up Toole's name on his computer screen. "Sure, in the Ducoing tomb. He's buried two down from my mom and daddy." He pointed, highlighting the spot on a map. He paused and looked up from the screen slyly. "That fella sure was a dunce, huh?"

The grave was on Latanier Avenue, a classy marble number with a cross above. Toole's name was sixth on the list of the buried, two above his mother's. The stone vases with DUCOING inscribed on them were empty. I plucked a clover that the riding lawnmower had spared and placed it on the stone.

When an author commits suicide, there's an urge to look back through his fiction for signs of trouble, for hints as to how his life will end. Toole left very few of those in *Confederacy*. His book is scathing, even sneering, but at the center of it is a sense of glee. I come away from its pages marveling at the weirdness around me, at the masquerade, rather than depressed by it. Even Ignatius, faced with his mother's threats to commit him to the mental hospital, gets a happy ending courtesy of his beatnik quasi ex-girlfriend, that "musky minx" Myrna Minkoff. She appears at his doorstep just before the ambulance from Charity Hospital does, and the two of them, loaded with Ignatius's lute and loose-leaf papers, head to New York:

> Myrna prodded and shifted the Renault through the city traffic masterfully, weaving in and out of impossibly narrow lanes until they were clear of the last twinkling streetlight of the last swampy suburb. Then they were in darkness in the center of the salt marshes. Ignatius looked out at the highway marker that reflected their headlights. U.S. 11. The marker flew past. He rolled down the window an inch or two and breathed the salt air blowing in over the marshes from the Gulf. As if the air was a purgative, his valve opened. He breathed again, this time more deeply. The dull headache was lifting.

The party doesn't end, it just moves. I wished that Toole's life could have had a similar deus ex machina, a journey that ended somewhere other than that lonely Biloxi highway.

8. Barry Hannah and Larry Brown's Fishing Spot
OXFORD, MS

I finished my journey by winding my way from Louisiana back up through Mississippi to return to Oxford, that town where Faulkner made his mark. Since his time there, Oxford has ushered in a new generation of fiction writers, some drawn there by the University of Mississippi's MFA writing program, some by Faulkner's legacy.

THE OXFORD, MISSISSIPPI, of today is a place that William Faulkner would have had a hard time imagining. When I arrived, on a bleak February day, the courthouse square was in a semi-bustling state. A steady stream of college students filled the sidewalks, ambling between brunch and some leisurely studying. Stores selling bow ties and flip-flops, beer cozies and hair ribbons in red and navy, the college colors, lined the blocks downtown. A group of tourists snapped cell-phone photos with the bronze statue of Faulkner; someone had managed to lodge the last of a melting snowball in his hat. Floating above the square, beacon-like, was the town water tower, painted robin's-egg blue.

Bars with generously sized television screens for

watching football games have replaced the tucked-away juke joints, SUVs long ago replaced the mules and buggies, and blues music leaks out onto the pavement on weekend nights. On the way toward the square, I had stopped for coffee, biscuits, and gravy at Big Bad Breakfast, a restaurant with a twin vision of including pig products in every meal and naming dishes after Oxford writers. (Menu items include: Burgsalom, Burgsalom!, The Pel"egg"can Brief, The Secret History Omelet, and The High Lonesome—a tribute to Barry Hannah in steak and eggs.) The name of the place itself is a play on another Oxford luminary, Larry Brown, who wrote a collection titled *Big, Bad Love*. Oxford is now more hip college town than quaint backwater. In the past forty years, Faulkner's postage stamp has expanded into a cultural destination.

It was a slow and deliberate change from the Oxford of the 1960s into the place I arrived at. In the early 1970s, the University of Mississippi was mostly known for the anti-integration riots after James Meredith became the first black student admitted to the school. Reclaiming Faulkner became a way to reimagine the town and its community. In 1973, just a decade after Faulkner's death, a group of academics founded the Faulkner and Yoknapatawpha conference, which expanded into an annual program of lectures and presentations on his work. After Faulkner's widow, Estelle, died in 1977, the University of Mississippi purchased Rowan Oak, restored the estate, and opened the home to visitors. Ole Miss rolled out a Southern Studies program, founded the Center for the Study of Southern Culture, and started beefing up its Creative Writing Department.

The first place I set off for in the square is the first stop I take on every visit: Square Books, a shop yearly in contention for the best independent bookstore in the South, if not the country. Longtime Oxford resident Richard Howorth and his wife, Lisa, established Square Books in 1979, and have worked to make it a literary hub—a well-curated, friendly place where out-of-towners flock on their way through town. Literary heavyweights began to read there, and it became a hangout for the bookish parties of the town. It became popular enough that the Howorths opened two more stores on the square: Square Books, Jr., dedicated to children's literature, and Off Square Books, for used and remaindered copies. Richard Howorth even served as mayor of Oxford from 2001 to 2009. And he was also a close friend and booster of many of the writers who lived or pass through Oxford. One of them was a minor literary celebrity who joined University of Mississippi as the writer-in-residence in 1983, a man who would spend many afternoons with a dog-eared copy of a novel on the balcony of Square Books: Barry Hannah.

HANNAH WAS A native Mississippian. He was born in Meridian and grew up in the tiny town of Clinton, a dozen miles northwest of Jackson, in 1942. Clinton is now part of the Jackson metropolitan area, but at the time Hannah was growing up, it was a peaceful, conservative hamlet. Hannah's father was a banker turned insurance salesman. His mother, a devout Baptist, brought Hannah to services, where he soaked up the rhythm of scripture and learned the chatter of the congregants by heart. "I see them pass still, the little old tiny-headed women of Clinton, Mississippi, in the '50s, in their giant cars on the brick street," Hannah wrote in an essay for the *Oxford American*. "They established the tone of my world."

His first foray into creative writing was thanks to a third-grade teacher who allowed Hannah to turn in little written stories in lieu of his actual assignments. "The fact is I wanted to write long before I had anything to say," Hannah later wrote. He enrolled at Mississippi College, also in Clinton, as a pre-med major, but switched to literature after discovering the work of Ernest Hemingway and Henry Miller. An MFA in fiction at the University of Arkansas soon followed, and his time out of his home state had the effect of solidifying his fondness for Mississippi. "I'll only say that I became more committed to people who could never tell their own stories," Hannah wrote. "And that I was no longer ashamed of being from the most derided state in the Union."

By the time he moved back to Oxford as a writer-in-residence, Hannah was already well established as master of darkly comic, gripping fiction. His twisted coming-of-age novel *Geronimo Rex* was nominated for the National Book Award in 1973, and established Han-

nah as part of a new wave of Southern writers whose
work had absorbed the rich literary traditions of the
area but had gone for something wilder. In it you can
sense the quiet intensity of Flannery O'Connor and
the razzle-dazzle descriptive power of Truman Capote,
but only as you might recognize ancestral features on a
newborn's face. Hannah's work was all his own, infused
with Southern wit and weirdness.

His writing in *Rex* fairly crackles with electricity.
Hannah has a knack for making his sentences veer suddenly into unexpected territory, sometimes teetering
on the brink of jumbled incoherence. His writing is a
high-wire act: There's a daredevil quality to his prose,
always a sense of risk involved. At its worst, *Rex* seems
oversaturated, unwieldy and reckless, too many fire-
works crammed into one display. But at its best, it's just
plain thrilling, explosive and impassioned and spell-
binding stuff. As when the protagonist Harry Monroe
describes his first encounter with the Dream of Pines
marching band: "This band was the best music I'd ever
heard, bar none. They made you want to pick up a rifle
and just get killed somewhere." Or Monroe's unsenti-
mental assessment of his drive home from college on
Christmas break: "I passed the fields like dead palo-
mino horses—winterset in Mississippi—the sun a cold
bulb; and later, over the Vicksburg bridge, saw the river:
a snake in throes, its belly up." His assessment of one of
his conquests: "Her voice was as thin as an ill-poached
egg thrown against the treble strings of a harp." Han-

nah knew how to mix Southern vernacular into his language in a way that seems exact rather than hokey. In the pages of *Rex*, men slosh into rooms, people put on their shoes "contrariwise," and barrels get "tumped" over. Hannah revels in the sheer possibility of those words, their sounds, but he makes the slang essential rather than decorative.

Inside the entrance of Square Books, just next to the stairs, is a wall of books by local authors, Hannah featured prominently. It's easy to understand why he liked the place; anyone who has an itch for the written word would. Copies of classics mingled with recent bestsellers, and posters advertised the authors who would be shortly passing through. The Faulkner-dedicated section is upstairs, by the café. The wall next to the stairs is cluttered with signed pictures of authors, including a large photo of Hannah, posing in sunglasses in front of the courthouse, grinning. Behind the counter, bumper stickers for sale proclaimed, I'D RATHER BE READING *AIRSHIPS*.

Hannah had followed *Rex* with the positively reviewed novel *Nightwatchmen*, but his status as a cult writer was cemented with the 1978 short-story collection *Airships*. The collection introduced themes that would run throughout his writing: airplanes, women, motorcycles, old Confederates spinning tall tales, fishing trips, and sudden outbursts of violence. Short stories provided range for Hannah's voice, good containers for its elegance and intensity. His literary pyrotechnics are grouped into short, entrancing bursts, but the stories are more than just stylistic hot-dogging. There are undertones of melancholy and menace; sentences inside the stories serve as perfectly encapsulated stories themselves. Like this one, from "Love Too Long":

> She and the architect were having fancy drinks together at a beach lounge when his ex-wife from New Hampshire showed up naked with a single-shotgun gun that was used in the Franco-Prussian War—it was a quaint piece hanging on the wall in their house when he was at Dartmouth—and screaming.

Like Flannery O'Connor and Harry Crews, Hannah favored titles that were also microstories, like "Midnight and I'm Not Famous Yet," a phrase Hannah's pal Jimmy Buffett later lifted for a song of his, or the later "Hey, Have You Got a Cig, the Time, the News, My Face?"

With *Airships* and his novel *Ray* Hannah became a writer whom other writers admired. Reviewers hailed him as a Southern version of Charles Bukowski. Robert Altman recruited Hannah to be a writer in Hollywood, an ultimately ill-fated experiment. "Turns out, I'm not a good screenwriter," Hannah noted wryly. Truman Capote became a fervent fan of his, labeling Hannah "the maddest writer in the U.S.A." Hunter S. Thompson, in a blurb, gave a gonzo compliment that Hannah often repeated: "Hannah should not be in front of young people. And perhaps he should be in a cage."

If these phrases sound like Hannah's own version of the famous description of Lord Byron, "mad, bad and dangerous to know," it's because his reputation was not solely based on his feats of literary prowess. During stints as a writing teacher at the Iowa Writers' Workshop, Middlebury, Texas State University, and the University of Montana at Missoula, Hannah had become notorious for his bad behavior, often fueled by booze. His fondness for alcohol and guns contributed to an image of Hannah as an off-kilter loon with a taste for explosive situations.

One story has Hannah firing a rifle into the floor of his car in order to drain accumulated rainwater. When he needed to make a hole in his wall to run stereo wires through it, he blasted away with a shotgun. At the University of Alabama in Tuscaloosa, Hannah landed a tenured teaching position, but the five years he was there coincided with a particularly chaotic time in his personal life. He drank heavily, and he and his second wife divorced. "It was probably the saddest time in my life," he noted later. He was fired after bringing a revolver into one of his classrooms, using the six chambers as a way to illustrate structuring a short story into six movements, and then waving the gun into the air when students tried to walk out on him. "A lot of that stuff was not a good idea, but it gets turned around by middle-class minds into a cowboy thing,'" Hannah told the *New York Times*. "It wasn't. It was just a need to find something real, to do something that was real."

When he landed in Oxford, a town that he later described as "a United Nations with catfish on its breath," Hannah swiftly became part of the town's lore. He had a fondness for motorcycles and flashy outfits; the sight of him whipping through the square on his chopper soon became a familiar part of the landscape. Even in his later days, when his health had deteriorated, Hannah would pull up to Square Books on his motorcycle, his oxygen tank in tow. The writer Darcey Steinke recalled Hannah's proclivity for spending Saturdays reclining on a lawn chair while wearing just a Speedo, drinking martinis and throwing the emptied glasses against the trash can.

"You know, all my heroes were alcoholics: Joyce, Hemingway, Faulkner. How many more do you want?" Hannah said in an interview with Wells Tower for *The Believer*. "The alcohol had the code and mystery about it as a writer's drug, but I'm glad that's been debunked. But the trouble with the drinking, much as I hate to admit it, is it helped the work. The first two drinks were always wonderfully liberating. You think better. You're braver, and you'll say anything. If you could just hang in there with two or three, it'd be beautiful. The trouble was I couldn't."

————

SHORTLY AFTER BARRY Hannah settled into town, he met Larry Brown. An ex-Marine from Yocona, a small community just south of Oxford, Brown started developing literary ambitions in his late twenties. He favored a uniform of work jeans and cowboy boots. His accent, a patient hill-country drawl, was so thick that Hannah later had to translate it for a French publisher who was perfectly fluent in English. He joined the Oxford Fire Department at twenty-two after leaving the armed forces, working odd jobs between shifts to help support his family. (His time in the firehouse would later inspire a memoir, *On Fire*.) "When I was twenty-nine, I stopped and looked at my life and wondered if I was ever going to do anything with it," Brown recounted in an essay. "I guess what I thought for most of my life was that I'd just let one day take care of the next. I'd made it that way okay for a long time, had some good times, some beautiful babies. But those babies were going to grow up. They were going to want things, and I wanted things to be better for them than they had been for me."

When Brown first approached Hannah with some of his unpublished stories, Hannah was outwardly encouraging but privately skeptical of Brown's writing career. "He showed me stories that were so bad, I'd duck out the back of the bar when I saw him coming down the walk with his inevitable manila envelope," Hannah wrote. "I couldn't stand hurting his feelings. I loved his sincerity.

I didn't give him a cold prayer in hell as to a future in literature."

But it was the beginning of a long friendship, cemented, for Brown, by Hannah's relationship with Harry Crews. In an essay about his friendship with Hannah, Brown remembers Hannah leading him over to a wall in his house where a picture of Crews was hanging, an author who Brown wrote was "my own personal candidate for Great Writer of the Century." As part of his new writing career, Brown had upped his already voracious reading appetite, and found Crews's work and tenacity especially encouraging. "I knew that back in those days when he was unpublished, he must have wanted success as badly as I did then," Brown wrote in a tribute to Crews. "It meant that I was not the only person who had ever gone through what I was enduring, that it was probably a universal experience, this apprenticeship period, this time when you wrote things that were not good only to throw them away or have them rejected in order to write enough to eventually learn how."

Thanks to a steady diet of books and pure trial and error, Brown's apprenticeship paid off. He had begun hanging out at Square Books and gave Richard Howorth some of his recent work, which impressed Howorth enough that he began to help Brown place his stories with magazines and publishers. The difference was a shift from experimenting with thrillers and horror stories—one of Brown's earliest attempts was about a man-eating bear at Yellowstone—to something closer to home, the rhythms and social worlds of Northern Mississippi. "I wasted a lot of time writing about things I didn't know anything about," Brown wrote. "You don't know when you start out that there's plenty of life around you, no matter where you live."

Brown had his first book reading at Square Books in 1988, around the same time that another Oxford native, John Grisham, was also celebrating his debut novel at the store. Grisham wrote a note to Brown in 1989, saying, "I hope you sell a million copies. And if you do, and if I sell a million copies of *A Time to Kill,* then maybe we can retire to the balcony at Square Books and spend our time drinking cold beer, watching co-eds, and talking about future books." As I combed through the shelves of Square Books, I noticed a photo of Brown hung right beside one of Hannah. He was holding a beer and grinning shyly, as if in sly triumph.

From Square Books, I walked over to City Grocery, just two doors down from the bookstore, through a crowd of hungover-looking students clad in fleece jackets and khaki shorts. The restaurant was beginning to fill up with lunch customers eagerly awaiting their weekend catfish creole or some of the superlative house shrimp and grits. The upstairs portion of the place is a bar, all polished wood and high-backed stools, where Brown would spend most of his evenings, and Hannah would sometimes entertain students or visitors. (An apocryphal Hannah story has him bringing his fishing pole to the balcony of City Grocery in an attempt to hook the hats of passersby.) Like most bars, the inside of City Grocery was less impressive than the stories that came out of it. Hannah would relax on the balcony and people watch, throwing out zingers to his companion. Brown would go to sop up the conversation and drink peach schnapps chased with Budweiser or Crown Royal, his favorite combination. "It's just like, a natural thing to set a story in the bar because that's where I spend so much of my life, at a bar. That's where I hang out with my friends," Brown said in an interview.

Like Hannah, Brown struggled with drinking. "I write by binges and I drink by binges," he told a reporter from *USA Today*. "But it's not good to try to write and drink at the same time." The drinking and the time shut away from his family put a strain on his marriage. At City Grocery, his wife, Mary Annie, whom Brown called M.A., would try to lure Brown away from the bar as he pleaded for "just one more," a phrase that Mary Annie joked would be the title of her own book. "I'll just put it this way," Mary Annie told Gary Hawkins, the director of *The Rough South of Larry Brown*, "I thought he wasted a lot of hours. Now, he might not have thought so, but he did. And he wasted a lot of mine." Or, as Hannah put it in his remembrance, Brown "was not a saint and we should remember that to their wives all men are garbage men trying to make a comeback."

FROM THE SQUARE, I aimed my car south, toward the tiny farming town of Yocona and the adjacent community of Tula, where Brown had spent most of his life. The places along the highway have names derived from the Chickasaw tribe that first lived there; "Yocona" roughly translates to "the places of the earth." In Tula, Brown had bought a patch of land around a pond that he used to fish in as a boy. On the eight acres of land, he had built a boat dock, cleaned out the pond, and restocked it with catfish, crappie, and bass. It became a place of respite for Brown and his family, a getaway spot where friends would come to camp and fish and hang out in warmer weather. Hannah was one of the frequent visitors to Brown's pond, where the two would kick back and fish. After Brown's death of a heart attack in 2004, Hannah would sometimes bring friends and interviewers along with him to the pond at Tula, to pay his respects.

In Tula, Brown's grand project had been to build a little writing cabin just on the shore of the pond, a place away from the main building where he could sit and go on a long writing binge amidst the scenery he loved. I had asked Mary Annie for permission to go see Brown's writing cabin, and she had sent me directions to navigate the winding roads to get there. "Enjoy our peaceful place," she told me. Shane, Brown's younger son, had recently moved onto the property. His eldest, Billy Ray, operates a dairy farm down the road, the inspiration for Brown's book of essays *Billy Ray's Farm*. You can buy the farm's milk at the market in town. I passed the sign for the farm on the way, and caught a glimpse of cows roaming in the adjacent field, huddled together. The bright February sky was streaked with graying clouds, reminding me of a passage that Brown wrote in his memoir *On Fire*:

> I live out in the county, out here in the land of the Big Sky country. I live at the edge of a river bottom and the clouds can go all mushroomy and marshmallowy late in the afternoon and loom up big and white in the sky so that they can capture your attention.

After several turns, I came to an iron gate that had A PLACE CALLED TULA forged onto the top. I opened the gate and drove through, down the truck tracks that served as a driveway, and parked near the main cabin, a sea-foam green building with a generous back porch. Two Adirondack chairs in disrepair populated a boat dock; beside them sat a Cool Whip container filled with fishing lures. An iron bottle tree bedecked with faded red, yellow, and blue empties stood nearby. Brown's headstone was on the far side of the pond. He's buried next to his daughter, Delinah, who died shortly after birth.

The pond itself was a dark, sludgy green, partly iced over from the recent freeze. The sweet gums lining the pond were skeletons; their leaves formed a thick, mottled brown carpet around the water, contrasting with the bright needles of the pine trees interspersed throughout the woods. I walked around the pond slowly toward the tiny writing shack on the other side, listening to the rustle of squirrels, the occasional echoing bird-call. Caught fishing line flashed in the trees; the leaves hissed and crackled beneath my boots. Even in the cold, it wasn't hard to imagine a warmer day not too many years ago when Hannah and Brown would have cast their lines into the water together and swapped tales.

In every collection, Hannah included a fishing story. The rhythms of baiting a hook, waiting for a bite, and reeling in a catch appealed to Hannah, made a kind of parallel to his writing process. Unlike Crews and Brown, Hannah didn't write by committing himself to sitting in front of a typewriter for a certain number of hours every day. When stories struck, they struck, and Hannah would write them as quickly as he could. In his collection *Captain Maximus*, Hannah started the story "Getting Ready" with the line: "He was forty-eight, a fisherman, and he had never caught a significant fish." The protagonist, Roger Laird, ends up selling his equipment at a loss, building a pair of stilts, and wading out into the lake to scream obscenities at the people passing in sailboats. In Hannah's most famous fishing story, "Water Liars," from *Airships*, men grapple with the sexual drives of women over their rods and reels. "When I am run down and flocked around by the world, I go down to Farte Cove off the Yazoo River and take my beer to the end of the pier where the old liars are still snapping and wheezing at each other," Hannah begins. Out in Tula, Brown and Hannah were part of the snapping and wheezing crowd.

A little wooden walkway spans a short ravine leading up to the cabin, with a sign in purple and white letters that reads, simply, THE SHACK. The cabin had a small porch with a rusting chair on it, providing a vantage point to overlook the pond. Inside, the walls were painted bright red, an African mask glared from its hook on the wall, and a chandelier of candle holders hung from the ceiling.

Like his writing career, the little shack was the fruit of Larry Brown's sheer doggedness, a willingness to work hard and face rejection and work out the problems in the process over and over. His love for the place where he lived informed his work, his legacy, and his construction projects. "Loggers and housewives and children and drunks and farmers and mailmen and lawyers and widowed old ladies and mechanics and cowboys and bums and preachers, every one of them has a story, and I know now that the little place I live in is full of stories," Brown wrote. "I don't think I'll ever tire of writing about them. There's too much beauty in the world that I know, about ten miles out of Oxford, Mississippi."

If that sounds like Faulkner's "postage stamp," it's not a coincidence. Brown had grown up with Faulkner as a local muse; he had started reading Faulkner's writing as a teenager, and became familiar with the grounds of Rowan Oak thanks to the fire department. The fire-alarm system there, he wrote in *On Fire*, "is sensitive enough that a bug can walk inside it and set it off, but still the trucks have to roll." Brown began rereading Faulkner's novels with purpose, sometimes strolling the grounds of Rowan Oak just to marvel at the place, and walk around the trees. Brown kept two pieces of cloth from Faulkner's favorite chair, one hung above his typewriter, and one in his pocket.

Unlike Brown, Hannah's relationship with Faulkner was an uneasy one. Even if Hannah's work hadn't previously drawn comparisons to Faulkner before he moved to Oxford—and, as a Mississippian, it inevitably had—it became inescapable. "When I first came here, I just heard Faulkner Faulkner Faulkner. His kinfolk and all of it—I was just bored by it. But then I grew to like to have these ghosts around," he told the *Believer*. "I find it amenable."

But I don't know that I believe Hannah; the relationship was more complicated than that. In the Oxford Hannah knew, Faulkner had become as much a brand as a scribe, a name slapped on events and items to sell them as highbrow and literary. Faulkner inherited the burden of the South's past, and then became part of the burden, at least for writers trying to craft original work in his shadow. Faulkner, the persona and not the writing, became part of the prevailing tropes applied to someone living in the South with literary ambitions—the "canned dream of the South," as Hannah put it.

The high-octane metaphors in works like *Airships* read like efforts to gain enough power to bust out of Faulkner's orbit, to redefine the idea of a Southern writer.

Faulkner's writing also seemed to weigh heavily on Hannah's ambitions. "I think of those moments in Faulkner, Beckett, and Holy Scripture, when the words seem absolutely final, bodiless, unattached, as out of a cloud of huge necessity," Hannah wrote. "My desire is to come even close to that team—to be that lucky, to be touched by such grace." Hannah often spoke about how his prose fell short of his intentions, was something that he felt a sense of disappointment about. In one interview, he confessed that he could barely stand to read his books over again. "You've got that dream, that gemlike flame you want to apply to something you've seen or something that's been in your heart a long time, and the first sentence murders it," Hannah told the *Oxford American*. "It breaks your heart a little. I understand that Muslims would put a deliberate imperfection into the pictures they created because only God was perfect. Well, I don't have that trouble."

I think of that often when I read Hannah, that gemlike flame and the idea of the written word constantly failing him. To me, Hannah is one of those writers whose grasp on language makes you doubt that you have the same common pool of vocabulary. His sentences are so deft and unpredictable, his characters rich and bizarre and precise. His failure to have written the Bible or *The Sound and the Fury* reads as something like The Rolling

Stones' failure to be Muddy Waters: Hannah could not help but write as himself, and the world is richer for it. The opening of Hannah's novel *Ray* always felt to me like a rebuke of the scene between Quentin Compson and his roommate in *Absalom, Absalom!*, the one where he keeps asking what it is about the South that haunts Quentin so. In *Ray*, a professor responds forcefully to a poem by his student: "They always say Southerners can write. So I slugged this skinny lad. I laid him down the steps . . . his family is saying they'll sue."

After he died of a heart attack in 2010, Hannah was even buried in the same cemetery as Faulkner, his own marble tombstone is just a hundred feet away down the hill from Faulkner's. Instead of bottles of Four Roses, Hannah's admirers leave toy guns and highlighters on the grave. Inscribed in the stone is a quote from his story "Escape to Newark," one of the gems in *Airships*: "It was a short ride, like all the best ones."

Coda

BEFORE I LEFT OXFORD, I swung by Square Books one last time to grab a coffee before the long drive home and idly leaf through the riches there. Richard Wright, Flannery O'Connor, Eudora Welty, Harry Crews, Truman Capote, Harper Lee, John Kennedy Toole, and, of course, William Faulkner: all of the people whose homes I visited were amply represented. It was amazing to see, all these literary treasures from a place once forsaken as a cultural desert. There was a time when being from the South meant that you couldn't put pen to paper; now it means that you're imbued with a mysterious writerly spirit. It's not just Square, either: The South has many of these marvelous places, these little bookstores that serve as hubs for a literary community and champions for writers. In Jackson, I sometimes head to Lemuria Books on my way back from the airport, sometimes taking time to glance in the back where the signed copies of Faulkner and O'Connor are nestled in with first editions of *Airships* and Larry Brown's *Dirty Work*. In New Orleans, there's Faulkner House Books in the French Quarter and Maple Street Book Store Uptown, just a block away from where John Kennedy Toole and his mother lived; Maple Street's owner, Rhoda Faust, was one of the people who worked with Thelma Toole and Walker Percy to get *Confederacy of Dunces* published. In Birmingham, there's the stately Alabama Booksmith and college student hangout The Little Professor, both places I spent many afternoons in browsing. In Atlanta, there's the cozy A Capella Books, a gold mine for out-of-print titles; in Nashville, the airy and inviting Parnassus Books; and in Asheville, the nicely curated Malaprop's Bookstore and Café.

I still don't entirely know what it is exactly about the South that inspired so many great writers to labor over it. But I think I have a better idea now. I lingered over the shelves full of local and Southern writers. Though the sites I had visited had, with one exception, been tied to writers who had died, the Southern literary tradition is far from dead, as those shelves teeming with new entries, from Ron Rash's *The Cove* to Dorothy Allison's *Bastard Out of Carolina*, proved. New writers have decided to stake out claims on their own tiny patches of earth—authors like Jesmyn Ward, whose aching novel *Salvage the Bones* focused on a family in rural Mississippi in the days before Katrina, Thomas Pierce, a Charlottesville-based writer of nimble, finely wrought stories, and Ann Pancake, a vibrant chronicler of Appalachian America. Each of them, it seemed to me, were talking to one another across time and style and subject matter. It was a vast conversation about the region, the creatures that lived there, the mannerisms and myths that became entwined with the place. The South is not just the setting; it's the soul of the thing. It comes with a fraught history, with accents and anxieties, with expectations and mythologies to contend with. Southern literature is about preservation, marking out the idiosyncrasies that distinguish the region from others, and it is also about a kind of controlled destruction, constantly replacing the idea of the place with the concrete details of it. It is an ongoing cartographic exercise, to trace and retrace the boundaries of the South, to try to figure out what it contains. It's about figuring out just where exactly you are. It's about going home.

Acknowledgments

Thanks to Matt Weiland, a deft and insightful editor whose continual encouragement helped me through many a rough patch. Thanks to the endlessly patient and conscientious Sam MacLaughlin, who worked out many a line that had gone cattywampus. Thanks also to my excellent copyeditor, Rachelle Mandik, and to the entire team at Norton.

Thanks to my agent, Brandi Bowles, and my editors at *The Paris Review Daily*, Deirdre Foley-Mendelssohn and Sadie Stein, who published an early version of the chapter on Eudora Welty and helped shape the idea for this book.

I am indebted to the many people who helped with my research, particularly Susan Haltom, Don Haselden, Ted Geltner, Mary Alice Welty White, Cory MacLauchlin, Craig Amason, Erik Bledsoe, Suzanne Marrs, Mary Annie Brown, and Sally Wolff-King. Thanks to Anna Hartford, a keen-eyed and generous first reader. To the friends and family who sheltered me, fed me, joined me on my journeys, offered me whiskey and advice, took care of my ornery cats, listened to me wax endless on the virtues and vices of Southern writers, read scraps of my drafts, and otherwise put up with me during these book-writing years—my brothers Conor and Brendan, my sister-in-law Susan, Katie Porter, Susan Colvin, Winston Bell, Lorianna Baker, Nick Russell, Eliza Lloyd, Lucas Adams, Will Dizard, Andrew Martin, Jared Miller, Anne Epstein, Rachel Apatoff, Aja Hazelhoff, Beth Stebner, Laurie Kamens, Jessica Loudis, and Eli Goldfarb—I can't thank you enough.

My teachers at the Altamont School in Birmingham got me hooked on Southern literature at a young age, in particular Jim Palmer, brave or foolish enough to teach Faulkner to a class of know-nothing eighth-graders, and Jimmy Wiygul, who took a busload of seventeen-year-olds on our first literary pilgrimage.

If anyone can be blamed for aiding this bibliophilia of mine, it has to be my wonderful parents, Tom and Mary. I am unendingly grateful for their love, support, and reluctance to stop me from reading at the dinner table.

Notes

Introduction

12   **"What is it? Something you live and breathe in . . ."** William Faulkner, *Absalom, Absalom!* (Knopf Doubleday, 2011), 289.

13   **"canned dream of the South,"** "Barry Hannah in Conversation with Wells Tower," *The Believer*, October 2010.

13   **"I have found that anything . . ."** Flannery O'Connor, *Mystery and Manners* (Farrar, Straus and Giroux, 1969), 40.

1. Eudora Welty's Garden

19   **"locally underfoot"** Peggy Whitman Prenshaw, ed., *Conversations with Eudora Welty* (University Press of Mississippi, 1984), 214.

19   **"It's where I live and look around . . ."** Ibid., 134.

21   **"A place that ever was lived in . . ."** Eudora Welty, *Some Notes on River Country* (University Press of Mississippi, 1944), 7.

22   **"When I ask company to dinner . . ."** Letter from Eudora Welty to William Maxwell, August 20, 1981, in *What There Is to Say We Have Said: The Correspondence of Eudora Welty and William Maxwell*, ed. Suzanne Marrs (Houghton Mifflin Harcourt, 2011), 373.

23   **"on tiptoe"** Diana Trilling, "Fiction in Review," *The Nation*, May 1946.

24   **" 'Regional,' I think, is a careless . . ."** Eudora Welty, "Place in Fiction," in *The Eye of the Story: Selected Essays and Reviews* (Vintage, 1990), 132.

25   **"a naked, luminous . . ."** Eudora Welty, *The Golden Apples* (Houghton Mifflin Harcourt, 1956), 267.

26   **"The sight of the garden . . ."** Manuscript draft of *One Writer's Beginnings*, the Eudora Welty Collection, Mississippi Department of Archives and History.

26   **"set myself at . . ."** Jane Roy Brown and Susan Haltom, *One Writer's Garden: Eudora Welty's Home Place* (University Press of Mississippi, 2011), x.

27   **"oak trees in little . . ."** Letter from Eudora Welty to William Maxwell, in Marrs, *What There Is to Say We Have Said*, 111.

27   **"buds as big as bobbins"** Ibid., 87.

27   **"We saw a TV . . ."** Ibid., 69.

27   **"I feel much greener"** Ibid., 171.

27   **"Here the thermometer . . ."** Ibid., 60.

29   **"She planted every kind . . ."** Eudora Welty, "A Curtain of Green," in *The Collected Stories of Eudora Welty* (Houghton Mifflin, 1982), 108.

30   **"Background matters . . ."** Eudora Welty, "The Art of Fiction No. 47," *The Paris Review*, Fall 1972.

30   **"[Southern writers] do not need . . ."** Eudora Welty, "Must the Novelist Crusade?," in *The Eye of the Story*, 156.

32   **"It's like sending . . ."** Welty, "The Art of Fiction No. 47."

33   **"One place comprehended . . ."** Eudora Welty, "On Writing," in *The Eye of the Story*, 128.

2. Richard Wright's Schoolhouse

37   **"Richard Wright's novel . . ."** Irving Howe, "Black Boys and Native Sons," in *Dissent* (University of Pennsylvania Press, 1963), 353.

37   **"How in hell . . ."** Hazel Rowley, *Richard Wright: The Life and Times* (University of Chicago Press, 2008), 250.

41   **"I never heard . . ."** Richard Wright, *Black Boy* (Harper Collins, 1993), 138.

42   **"the vague sense . . ."** Ibid.

43   **"It may seem like an insignificant . . ."** David S. Dreyer, "Natchez Is the Cradle of the South," *The Natchez Democrat*, February 9, 2009.

44   **"Hunger had always been . . ."** Wright, *Black Boy*, 14.

44   **"Were there, then, people . . ."** Ibid., 244.

44   **"I was jarred . . ."** Ibid., 248.

45   **"that gargantuan paradise . . ."** H. L. Mencken, "The Sahara of the Bozart," in *The American Scene: A Reader* (Knopf, 1988), 159.

45   **"In the North . . ."** Ibid., 161.

45   **"made him see his boss . . ."** Wright, *Black Boy*, 249.

46   **"I no longer** *felt* **. . ."** Ibid., 251.

48   **a dread of white people** . . . Ibid., 73.

48   **"The tale made . . ."** Ibid., 39.

49   **"I lived my childhood . . ."** Richard Wright, "Tradition and Industrialization," in *White Man, Listen!* (Harper-Perennial, 1957), 55.

51   **"I did not care if . . ."** Ibid., 178.

52   **"What I feel at the moment . . ."** Alice Walker, "Beyond the Peacock: The Reconstruction of Flannery O'Connor," in *Georgia Voices*, ed. Hugh M. Ruppersburg (University of Georgia Press, 1994), 436.

53   **"I was not leaving the South . . ."** Richard Wright, *Black Boy* (Harper and Bros, 1945), 277.

3. Faulkner's Liquor Cabinet

55   **"what needed to be said"** Letter from William Faulk-

ner to Richard Wright, 1945, in Hazel Rowley, *Richard Wright: The Life and Times* (University of Chicago Press, 2008), 324.

55 **"Dear Welty . . ."** Letter from William Faulkner to Eudora Welty, 1943, in Eudora Welty, *On William Faulkner* (University Press of Mississippi, 2003), 20.

55 **"living near a big mountain . . ."** Peggy Whitman Prenshaw, ed., *Conversations with Eudora Welty* (University Press of Mississippi, 1984), 80.

58 **"There's a black sheep . . ."** Dean Faulkner Wells, *Every Day by the Sun: A Memoir of the Faulkners of Mississippi* (Crown, 2011), 68.

58 **"As long as I live under . . ."** M. Thomas Inge, ed., *Conversations with William Faulkner* (University Press of Mississippi, 1999), 84.

58 **"Sue and be damned . . ."** Wells, *Every Day by the Sun*, 85.

60 **"Brother Will drank . . ."** Sally Wolff, ed., *Talking About William Faulkner* (Louisiana State University Press, 1996), 12.

60 **"The tools I need . . ."** William Faulkner, "The Art of Fiction No. 12," *Paris Review*, Spring 1956.

63 **"Beginning with *Sartoris* . . ."** Ibid.

64 **"gazed with empty eyes . . ."** William Faulkner, *The Sound and the Fury* (Knopf, 2011), 271.

64 **She's a particular expert . . .** This antebellum diary is a contentious subject among Faulkner scholars. It came to Wolff-King's attention through Mississippian Dr. Edgar Francisco Wiggins III, who claimed that his father was a close friend of Faulkner's. (Wolff-King published a book, *Ledgers of History*, that included Wiggins's childhood recollections of Faulkner as well as analysis connecting the text of Faulkner's work to

the diary.) But in 2014, journalist Maria Bustillos published an article on the Awl citing several academics skeptical of Wiggins's claims. They question whether there is sufficient evidence aside from his testimony to link the diary to Faulkner.

65 **"The deep South . . ."** William Faulkner, *Absalom, Absalom!* (Knopf, 2011), 4.

65 **"To live anywhere in . . ."** William Faulkner, "On Fear: The South in Labor," *Harper's*, June 1956.

66 **"Home again . . ."** William Faulkner, "Mississippi," *Holiday*, April 1954.

66 **"races like a dinosaur . . ."** Eudora Welty, "Looking at Short Stories," in *On Writing* (Random House, 2011), 25.

4. Flannery O'Connor's Peacocks

70 **"From that day with the Pathé man . . ."** Flannery O'Connor, "Living with a Peacock," *Holiday*, September 1961.

70 **"A gray bantam . . ."** Ibid.

70 **"a pidgeon-toed . . ."** Flannery O'Connor, "Biography," Flannery O'Connor Collection, Georgia College and State University.

72 **"going to Milledgeville"** Brad Gooch, *Flannery: A Life of Flannery O'Connor* (Little, Brown, 2009), 53.

72 **"We expect you . . ."** Letter from Flannery O'Connor to Maryat Lee, March 10, 1957, in *The Habit of Being*, ed. Sally Fitzgerald (Macmillan, 1988), 209.

72 **"Greetings from historic . . ."** Ibid., 220.

73 **"I was roped and tied . . ."** Ibid., 224.

73 **"Who was likely . . ."** Richard Gilman, "On Flannery O'Connor," *New York Review of Books*, August 21, 1969.

73   **"I stayed away . . ."** Letter from Flannery O'Connor to Cecil Dawkins, July 16, 1957, in Fitzgerald, *Habit*, 230.

76   **"I watch what goes on . . ."** Letter from Flannery O'Connor to Sally Fitzgerald, August 4, 1957, in Ibid., 234.

77   **"The lawn extended . . ."** Flannery O'Connor, "The Enduring Chill," *The Complete Stories of Flannery O'Connor* (Macmillan, 1971), 368.

80   **"He saw Jesus move from . . ."** Flannery O'Connor, *Wise Blood* (Macmillan, 2007), 16.

82   **"I have enough energy . . ."** Letter from Flannery O'Connor to Robert Lowell, March 17, 1953, in Fitzgerald, *Habit*, xvi.

82   **"It is hard to tell . . ."** O'Connor, "Living with a Peacock."

83   **"Visitors to our place . . ."** Ibid.

83   **"plowed all over . . ."** Letter from Flannery O'Connor to Cecil Dawkins, April 14, 1958, in Fitzgerald, *Habit*, 276.

84   **"You can't have a peacock . . ."** Letter from Flannery O'Connor to "A," November 25, 1955, in Ibid., 118.

85   **"a cheer for . . ."** O'Connor, "Living with a Peacock."

86   **"raking up feathers . . ."** Mark Jurgensen, "Snakebitten," andalusiafarm.blogspot.com, August 26, 2010.

88   **"I have a large . . ."** Letter from Flannery O'Connor to "A," June 1, 1956, in Fitzgerald, *Habit*, 161.

88   **"calls all the cows *he* . . ."** Letter from Flannery O'Connor to Sally Fitzgerald, September 1951, in Fitzgerald, *Habit*, 27.

89   **"eyes as blue as . . ."** Flannery O'Connor, "The Life You Save May Be Your Own," in *The Complete Stories of Flannery O'Connor*, 146.

89   **"Mary Flannery is . . ."** Gooch, *Flannery*, 278.

89   **"whose face was as broad . . ."** Flannery O'Connor, "A

Good Man Is Hard to Find," in *The Complete Stories of Flannery O'Connor*, 117.

90   **"unhappy combinations . . ."** Flannery O'Connor, "The Fiction Writer & His Country," in *Mystery and Manners* (Macmillan, 1969), 28.

90   **"We have become so flooded . . ."** Flannery O'Connor, "The Grotesque in Southern Fiction," in Ibid., 39.

92   **"I am always vastly irritated . . ."** Letter from Flannery O'Connor to Cecil Dawkins, July 16, 1957, in Fitzgerald, *Habit*, 230.

92   **"Because when she set . . ."** Alice Walker, "Beyond the Peacock: The Reconstruction of Flannery O'Connor," *Georgia Voices*, ed. Hugh M. Ruppersburg (University of Georgia Press, 1994), 431.

94   **"When we talk about . . ."** O'Connor, "The Fiction Writer & His Country," 34.

95   **"It is a great blessing . . ."** Flannery O'Connor, "The Regional Writer," in *Mystery and Manners* (Macmillan, 1969), 55.

5. Harry Crews's Hurricane Creek

98   **"a boy who was raised . . ."** Harry Crews, *A Childhood: The Biography of a Place*, in *Classic Crews: A Harry Crews Reader* (Simon & Schuster, 1993), 10.

100   **"I have never been able . . ."** Ibid., 14.

100   **"I am convinced . . ."** Joe David Bellamy, "Harry Crews: An Interview," reprinted in Erik Bledsoe, ed., *Getting Naked with Harry Crews* (University Press of Florida, 1999), 30–31.

103   a   **"G.-Gordon-Liddy-meets-Vanilla-Ice . . ."** "Harry Crews," *The Dennis Miller Show*, February 4, 1992, YouTube video posted by "mtheads," March 5, 2007, http://youtu.be/qpeFmXJG4Ak, accessed December 27, 2014.

104 "It's a psychological truth . . ." Ruth Ellen Rasche, "Blue-Eyed Boy," *University of Florida Today*, November 1992.

104 "Not many people *laugh* . . ." Erik Bledsoe, "Interview with Harry Crews," *Southern Quarterly*, 1998.

105 "I come from people . . ." Crews, *A Childhood*, in *Classic Crews*, 31.

111 "I have lived with the stories . . ." Ibid., 21.

112 "I reached over . . ." Ibid., 118.

113 "accept the good-natured brutality . . ." Ibid., 91.

114 "It was always the women . . ." Ibid., 101.

114 "unrelieved by humor . . ." Ibid., 101.

115 "rotten spot at the center . . ." Ibid., 31.

116 "I don't suppose you could . . ." Tom Graves, "An Interview with Harry Crews," in *Just Schools* (The Institute for Southern Studies, 1979), 151.

116 "so massive and so sudden . . ." Crews, *A Childhood*, in *Classic Crews*, 55.

118 "Willalee was our friend . . ." Ibid., 69.

120 "I was writing about people . . ." Interview with Harry Crews by Rodney Elrod, "The Freedom to Act," *New Letters*, Spring 1989.

121 "Since where we lived . . ." Crews, *A Childhood*, in *Classic Crews*, 67.

121 "What apprentices don't understand . . ." Al Burt, "Harry Crews: Working the Kinks Out," reprinted in Bledsoe, *Getting Naked*, 89.

6. Harper Lee and Truman Capote's Courthouse

128 "We are just going to feed . . ." Sharon Churcher, "Don't Mention the Mockingbird!" *The Mail Online*, June 26, 2010, www.dailymail.co.uk.

129 **"In rainy weather . . ."** Harper Lee, *To Kill a Mocking-bird* (Harper Collins, 2006), 5.

130 **"an island in a patchwork . . ."** Ibid., 174.

131 **"in character and . . ."** John K. Hutchens, "Life with Father," *New York Herald Tribune*, April 15, 1962.

131 **"It is and it isn't . . ."** Ibid.

136 **"Well, I didn't know . . ."** Gina Bellafante, "Harper Lee, Gregarious for a Day," *The New York Times*, January 30, 2006.

136 **"Boo was our neighbor . . ."** Lee, *Mockingbird*, 373.

137 **"If you know Boo . . ."** Oprah Winfrey in *Hey Boo: Harper Lee & To Kill a Mockingbird*, dir. Mary McDonagh Murphy, May 2011.

137 **"sundry sunless county cubbyholes . . ."** Lee, *Mockingbird*, 217.

138 **"When he played Atticus . . ."** Robert Mulligan, dir., *To Kill a Mockingbird*, Universal Legacy Series DVD, 2005.

138 **"I think it is one of . . ."** Bellafante, "Harper Lee, Gregarious for a Day."

140 **"I honestly think it would . . ."** Letter from Truman Capote to Mary Ida Faulk, December 5, 1959, Monroe County Heritage Museum.

140 **"Dill was . . ."** Lee, *Mockingbird*, 9.

141 **"Nelle's book . . ."** Letter from Truman Capote to Alvin and Marie Dewey, August 12, 1960, in *Too Brief a Treat: The Letters of Truman Capote,* ed. Gerald Clarke (Vintage, 2005), 286.

142 **"She is a gifted woman . . ."** George Plimpton, "The Story Behind a Nonfiction Novel," *The New York Times*, January 16, 1966.

142 **"Those people had . . ."** Gary Jarmer, "In Cold Blood: An American Tragedy," *Newsweek*, January 24, 1966.

142 **"A Kansas paper said . . ."** Plimpton, "The Story Behind a Nonfiction Novel."

144 **"Both times she was . . ."** Gerald Clarke, *Capote: A Biography* (Simon & Schuster, 2010), 22.

144 **"It was a fabrication of . . ."** "Lee Says Drowning Story False," Associated Press, September 25, 1997.

144 **"liked it very much . . ."** Capote to Faulk, July 9, 1959.

146 **"It's always the same . . ."** Truman Capote, *A Christmas Memory* (Knopf, 2006), 3.

147 **"There was no hurry . . ."** Lee, *Mockingbird*, 6.

148 **"The one thing that doesn't . . ."** Ibid., 140.

148 **"You never really understand . . ."** Ibid., 39.

148 **"It's interesting that all the folks . . ."** Letter from Flannery O'Connor to "A," October 1, 1960, in Sally Fitzgerald, ed., *The Habit of Being* (Macmillan, 1988), 411.

149 **"As you know . . ."** Roy Newquist, *Counterpoint* (Rand McNally, 1964), 412.

151 **"I don't do anything . . ."** Ben Raines, "Alice Lee, Sister of Author Harper Lee, Like 'Atticus Finch in a Skirt,'" *The Birmingham News*, June 10, 2011.

152 **"The notion that a writer . . ."** Kay Bonnett, "An Interview with Harry Crews," reprinted in Erik Bledsoe, ed., *Getting Naked with Harry Crews* (University Press of Florida, 1999), 166.

154 **"I have no obligations . . ."** David Shields and Shane Salerno, *Salinger* (Simon & Schuster, 2013), 101.

7. John Kennedy Toole's Hot-Dog Carts

159 **"Each time I sent . . ."** Cory MacLauchlin, *The Butterfly in the Typewriter* (Da Capo Press, 2012), 225.

160 **"Over the years . . ."** Walker Percy, foreword to John

Kennedy Toole, *A Confederacy of Dunces* (Grove, 1987), vii.

160 **"I don't know any novel . . ."** Letter from Walker Percy to Thelma Toole, December 1976, John Kennedy Toole Papers, Tulane University.

161 **"mother of the scholarly . . ."** MacLauchlin, *Butterfly*, 244.

161 **"I walk in the world . . ."** Typescript of interview with Tom Snyder, John Kennedy Toole Papers, Tulane University.

162 **"Gottlieb is . . ."** Mary Vespa, "A Much Rejected Novel Creates a Literary Sensation Thanks to an Indomitable Mother," *People*, September 22, 1980.

162 **"He had the seeing . . ."** "Thelma Toole Interview, 1983," YouTube video posted by The Center for New American Media Channel, October 16, 2013, http://youtu.be/dKsONW7UMsw, accessed December 27, 2014.

164 **"It is tempting . . ."** MacLauchlin, *Butterfly*, 216.

168 **"Irene, Reilly, Mancuso . . ."** Letter from John Kennedy Toole to Robert Gottlieb, March 5, 1965, Joel L. Fletcher Papers, Tulane University.

171 **"In the shadow . . ."** Toole, *Confederacy*, 1.

172 **"Docking a star . . ."** Yelp! listing for Ignatius J. Reilly Statue by "Jeff S.," http://www.yelp.com/biz/ignatius-j-reilly-statue-new-orleans, accessed February 16, 2014.

173 **"In the unreality . . ."** Toole to Gottlieb, March 5, 1965.

174 **"'I would like very much . . .'"** Toole, *Confederacy*, 42.

175 **"three different kinds . . ."** Joel Fletcher, *Ken and Thelma* (Pelican, 2005), 18.

175 **"like the April Fool . . ."** Ibid.

176 **"I've always resented . . ."** Ibid., 19.

176 **"I had hoped . . ."** Toole, *Confederacy*, 154.

176   **"I never read bestsellers"** Ibid., 48.

177   **"The book is not autobiography . . ."** Toole to Gott-lieb, March 5, 1965.

179   **"We must stay to watch . . ."** Toole, *Confederacy*, 17.

181   **"Our crew is still . . ."** Jerry Strahan, *Managing Igna-tius* (Broadway, 1999), xv.

182   **"the distinct odors . . ."** Toole, *Confederacy*, 152.

182   **"Rubber, cereal . . ."** Ibid., 153.

182   **"The wagon is a terrible . . ."** Ibid., 232.

183   **"made him look like a dinosaur . . ."** Ibid., 158.

186   **"two structures fused . . ."** Ibid., 82.

187   **"that dripped carving . . ."** Ibid., 36.

187   **"inhaled the moldy scent . . ."** Ibid., 35.

189   **"cacophony of dropping pots . . ."** Ibid., 266.

189   **"Poor Mr. Reilly . . ."** Ibid, 91.

190   **a screening of *Birth of a Nation* . . .** MacLauchlin, *But-terfly*, 113.

190   **"Technicolored horrors . . ."** Toole, *Confederacy*, 101.

192   **"extroverted and private"** René Pol Nevils and Debo-rah George Hardy, *Ignatius Rising* (LSU Press, 2005), 109.

195   **"Myrna prodded and shifted . . ."** Toole, *Confederacy*, 394.

8. Barry Hannah and Larry Brown's Fishing Hole

200   **"I see them pass . . ."** Barry Hannah, "Why I Write," *The Oxford American* 20, 1997.

200   **"The fact is I wanted . . ."** Ibid.

201   **"This band was the best . . ."** Barry Hannah, *Geronimo Rex* (Grove, 2007), 14.

201   **"I passed the fields . . ."** Ibid., 168.

201   **"Her voice was as thin . . ."** Ibid., 105.

203 **"She and the architect . . ."** Barry Hannah, "Love Too Long," in *Airships* (Grove, 2007), 12.

203 **"Turns out, I'm not . . ."** Barry Hannah, "The Art of Fiction No. 184," *The Paris Review,* Winter 2004.

204 **"It was probably . . ."** John Oliver Hodges, "VIDEO: Barry Hannah in Tuscaloosa," *The Oxford American,* March 9, 2011, http://www.oxfordamerican.org/articles/ 2011/mar/09/barry-hannah-tuscaloosa.

204 **"A lot of that stuff . . ."** Randy Kennedy, "At Home with Barry Hannah, Mellowing Out but Unbowed," *New York Times,* July 9, 1998.

205 **"a United Nations . . ."** Claire Howorth, "Writers Remember Barry Hannah," *Vanity Fair,* March 3, 2010, http://www.vanityfair.com/online/daily/2010/03/writers -remember-barry-hannah.

205 **Darcey Steinke recalled . . .** Darcey Steinke, "Barry Hannah and I," *The Millions,* October 13, 2014, http:// www.themillions.com/2014/10/hannah-and-i.html.

205 **"You know, all my heroes . . ."** "Barry Hannah in Conversation with Wells Tower," *The Believer,* October 2010.

206 **"When I was twenty-nine . . ."** Larry Brown, "Plenty to Write About," in *Dirty Work* (Algonquin, 2007), 241.

206 **"He showed me stories . . ."** Barry Hannah, "Introduction," in Larry Brown, *A Miracle of Catfish* (Algonquin, 2007), x.

207 **"my own personal candidate . . ."** Jean W. Cash, *Larry Brown: A Writer's Life* (University Press of Mississippi, 2011), 10.

207 **"I knew that . . ."** Larry Brown, *Billy Ray's Farm: Essays from a Place Called Tula* (Simon & Schuster, 2002), 20.

208 **"I wasted a lot of time . . ."** Brown, "Plenty to Write About.", 2.

208 **"I hope you sell . . ."** Cash, *Larry Brown,* 66.

209   **"It's just like . . ."** Jay Watson, ed., *Conversations with Larry Brown* (University Press of Mississippi, 2007), 157.

209   **"I write by binges . . ."** Bob Minzesheimer, "Remembering Larry Brown," *USA Today,* November 29, 2004.

209   **"I'll just put it this way . . ."** Gary Hawkins, "Just One More," *The Oxford American,* June 12, 2013.

209   **"was not a saint . . ."** Barry Hannah, "Introduction," ix.

211   **"I live out . . ."** Larry Brown, *On Fire* (Algonquin, 1994), 26.

212   **"He was forty-eight . . ."** Barry Hannah, "Getting Ready," in *Long, Last Happy: New and Selected Stories* (Grove, 2010), 107.

212   **"When I am run down . . ."** Barry Hannah, "Water Liars," in *Airships,* 3.

213   **"Loggers and housewives . . ."** Larry Brown, "A Late Start in Mississippi," *American Identities: Contemporary Multicultural Voices,* ed. Robert Pack and Jay Parini (UPNE, 1994), 33.

214   **"is sensitive enough . . ."** Brown, *On Fire,* 172.

214   **"When I first came here . . ."** "Barry Hannah in Conversation with Wells Tower."

214   **"canned dream . . ."** Ibid.

215   **"I think of those moments . . ."** Hannah, "Why I Write."

215   **"You've got that dream . . ."** Marc Smirnoff, "An Interview with Barry Hannah," *The Oxford American* 41, Fall 2001.

216   **"They always say . . ."** Barry Hannah, *Ray* (Grove, 2007), xiv.

Suggested Reading

Eudora Welty (1909–2001)

The first thing that I read and really loved by Eudora Welty was *The Optimist's Daughter*, a tightly packed novel about a woman coping with the death of her father and a house full of memories. For this book, I also had the pleasure of rereading many of Welty's short stories, such as the ever-hilarious "Why I Live at the P.O." and the aching "A Worn Path," which are both available in *The Collected Stories of Eudora Welty*. The work of Welty's biographer, Suzanne Marrs, was immensely helpful, and I particularly delighted in *What There Is To Say We Have Said: The Correspondence of Eudora Welty and William Maxwell*, which Marrs edited. Ditto the account of restoring Welty's garden put together by preservationist and garden designer Susan Haltom and landscape historian Jane Roy Brown, *One Writer's Garden: Eudora Welty's Home Place*. And for those who tell me that they aren't entranced by Welty's fiction, I always point to her brilliant collection *The Eye of the Story: Selected Essays and Reviews*, assessments and observations as interesting and sharp now as they were when Welty was writing them.

Richard Wright (1908–1960)

Richard Wright's powerful memoir, *Black Boy: A Record of Childhood and Youth*, was the inspiration for one of these chapters, and I highly recommend it. *Native Son* and *Uncle Tom's Children* are also natural choices, but Wright's publishing career went far beyond that. He wrote poetry (*Haiku: This Other World*) and many volumes of nonfiction and essays

(*White Man, Listen!* and *I Choose Exile* are both interesting reflections on the oppressions of racism and colonialism). For a biography of Wright, look to Hazel Rowley's excellent *Richard Wright: The Life and Times*.

William Faulkner (1897–1962)

The Sound and the Fury remains my favorite William Faulkner book; like most things he's written, it gets richer each time you read it. *Absalom, Absalom!* is a close second, and the first book of his I read was *The Unvanquished*, which is a good entry point if you normally shy away from stream-of-consciousness high modernism. Joseph Blotner's definitive *Faulkner: A Biography* was enormously helpful in getting a sense of the man, as was the deeply charming *Every Day by the Sun: A Memoir of the Faulkners of Mississippi* by his niece Dean Faulkner Wells. I would also strongly encourage a read of Faulkner's interview with *The Paris Review*, the source of many of his most famous quips, which is available online, bless them.

Flannery O'Connor (1925–1964)

Though I have a soft spot for her novels, especially *Wise Blood*, the volume that I keep coming back to by Flannery O'Connor is *The Complete Stories*, which has both her greatest hits ("A Good Man Is Hard to Find" and "Good Country People") and lesser-known gems ("Judgment Day" and "Greenleaf"). O'Connor's letters, collected and edited by her friend Sally Fitzgerald in *The Habit of Being: Letters of Flannery O'Connor*, are an absolute joy to read, and make me personally regret the invention of e-mail. Her wit and analysis are on full display in the essay and speeches collection *Mystery and Manners: Occasional Prose*, which captured her famous dictum about large and startling figures. Brad Gooch's biography *Flannery: A Life of Flannery O'Connor* was not only incredibly valuable to my research, it is also an absorbing read in itself, and I recommend it.

Harry Crews (1935–2012)

Many of Harry Crews's books are currently out of print, which is a damn shame, but the ones that you can get your hands on, you'd be well advised to read. My favorite, no secret, is his brutal memoir *A Childhood: The Biography of a Place*, which is packed neatly among the deeply weird novels *Car* and *The Gypsy's Curse* and three of Crews's essays in the edition *Classic Crews: A Harry Crews Reader*. Crews's harsh and haunting *A Feast of Snakes* will blow your lid off, as will his first novel, *The Gospel Singer*. And to get a taste of what Crews was like to interact with, look to the interview collection *Getting Naked with Harry Crews*, edited by Erik Bledsoe.

Harper Lee (b. 1926) and Truman Capote (1924–1984)

Harper Lee's most enduring work is her first one, *To Kill a Mockingbird*, though there aren't many to choose from. Luckily, there is no such lack of publication by Lee's childhood friend Truman Capote. *In Cold Blood* is the true crime novel that the two collaborated on, and well worth your time to peruse. My favorite essay of his is "A Christmas Memory," though his account of a little boy stuck in a decaying antebellum mansion in the novel *Other Voices, Other Rooms* is equally great. Capote's biographer, Gerald Clarke, published two go-to texts for my understanding of Capote's life, *Capote: A Biography* and the deliciously catty *Too Brief a Treat: The Letters of Truman Capote*.

John Kennedy Toole (1937–1969)

The posthumously published novel *A Confederacy of Dunces* is most of what we have from John Kennedy Toole, as well as *The Neon Bible*, the manuscript Toole wrote for a literary contest when he was sixteen. Cory MacLauchlin's biography *Butterfly in the Typewriter: The Tragic Life of John Kennedy Toole and the Remarkable Story of A Confederacy of Dunces*, is a well-researched and thoughtful account of Toole, and was instrumental to my research. Toole's friend Joel Fletcher also has a good account of the interaction between Toole and his mother in *Ken & Thelma: The Story of A Confederacy of Dunces*.

Barry Hannah (1942–2010) and
Larry Brown (1951–2004)

Where to start with Barry Hannah? *Airships*, most likely, but his short stories in *Captain Maximus* are equally excellent. If you haven't read any Hannah, the collection *Long, Last Happy*, which samples stories from throughout his publishing career, is worth picking up. His novella *Ray* is also worth your time, as is his first book *Geronimo Rex*. For this book, I also read and enjoyed *A Short Ride: Remembering Barry Hannah*, a collection of memories about Hannah from former students, friends, and colleagues. Larry Brown's short-story collection *Facing the Music* got me hooked, and *Big Bad Love* kept me on the line. Brown's essays in *Billy Ray's Farm* and his memoir *On Fire* give a good idea of the obstacles Brown overcame in his writing career, and his love of his pocket of North Mississippi. Jean W. Cash's *Larry Brown: A Writer's Life* was also a very instructive and interesting biography, and filled in some of the gaps left from Brown's memoirs.